The Power of Nonviolence

introduction by **Howard Zinn**

The Power of Nonviolence

writings

by advocates

of peace

Beacon Press

Boston

Beacon Press
25 Beacon Street
Boston, Massachusetts 02108-2892
www.beacon.org

Beacon Press books
are published under the auspices of
the Unitarian Universalist Association of Congregations.
© 2002 by Beacon Press
Introduction © 2002 by Howard Zinn
All rights reserved
Printed in the United States of America
06 05 04 03   8 7 6 5
This book is printed on acid-free paper that meets the uncoated paper
ANSI/NISO specifications for permanence as revised in 1992.
Text design by Julia Sedykh Design
Composition by Wilsted & Taylor Publishing Services
Library of Congress Cataloging-in-Publication Data
The power of nonviolence : writings by advocates of peace / introduction
by Howard Zinn ; [authors, Howard Zinn ... et al.].
p.   cm.
Originally published: Instead of violence / edited with notes and introductions
by Arthur and Lila Weinberg. New York : Grossman Publishers, 1963.
ISBN 0-8070-1407-9 (pbk. : alk. paper)
1. Peace. 2. Pacifism. 3. Nonviolence. I. Zinn, Howard [date]
JZ5538 .P685 2002
327.1'72—dc21
                                        2002018696

contents

Howard Zinn

Introduction: Retaliation

The images on television were heartbreaking. People on fire leaping to their deaths from a hundred stories up. People in panic and fear racing from the scene in clouds of dust and smoke. We thought that there must be thousands of human beings buried alive but soon dead under a mountain of debris. We imagined the terror among the passengers of the hijacked planes as they contemplated the crash, the fire, and the end.

Those scenes horrified and sickened me.

Then our political leaders came on television, and I was horrified and sickened again. They spoke of retaliation, of vengeance, of punishment.

"We are at war," they said. And I thought: they have learned nothing, absolutely nothing, from the history of the twentieth century, from a hundred years of retaliation, vengeance, war, a hundred years of terrorism and counter-terrorism, of violence met with violence in an unending cycle of stupidity.

We can all feel a terrible anger at whoever, in their insane idea that this would help their cause, killed thousands of innocent people. But what do we do with that anger? Do we react with panic, strike out violently and blindly just to show how tough we are? "We shall make no distinction," the President proclaimed, "between terrorists and countries that harbor terrorists." We bombed Afghanistan, and inevitably killed innocent people, because it is in the nature of bombing to be indiscriminate, to "make no distinction." Did we commit terrorist acts in order to "send a message" to terrorists?

We have responded that way before. It is the old way of thinking, the old way of acting, and it has never worked. Reagan bombed Libya, Bush made war on Iraq, and Clinton bombed Afghanistan and also a pharmaceutical plant in the Sudan, to "send a message" to terrorists. And then comes this horror in New York and Washington. Isn't it clear by now that sending a message to terrorists through violence doesn't work, it only leads to more terrorism?

Haven't we learned anything from the Israeli-Palestinian conflict? Car bombs planted by Palestinians bring tanks and air attacks by the Israeli government. That has been going on for years. It doesn't work, and innocent people die on both sides.

Yes, it is an old way of thinking, and we need new ways. We need to think about the resentment felt all over the world by people who have been the victims of American military action. In Vietnam, where we carried out terrorizing bombing attacks, using napalm and cluster bombs, on peasant villages. In Latin America, where we supported dictators and death squads in Chile, El Salvador, Nicaragua, and other countries. In Iraq, where a million people have died as a result of our economic sanctions. And perhaps most important for understanding the current situation, in the occupied territories of the West Bank and Gaza, where three million Palestinians live under a cruel military occupation, while the United States government supplies Israel with high-tech weapons.

We need to imagine that the awful scenes of death and suffering in New York, Washington, and Pennsylvania we witnessed on our television screens have been going on in other parts of the world for generations, and only now can we begin to know what people have gone through, often as a result of our policies. We need to understand how some of those people will go beyond quiet anger to acts of terrorism.

We need new ways of thinking. A $300 billion military budget has not given us security. American military bases all over the world, our warships on every ocean, have not given us security. Land mines and a "missile defense shield" will not give us security. We need to rethink our position in the world. We need to stop sending weapons to countries that oppress other people or their own people. We need to be resolute in our decision that we will not go to war, whatever reason is conjured up by the politicians or the media, because war in our time is always indiscriminate, a war against innocents, a war against children. War is terrorism, magnified a hundred times.

Our security can only come by using our national wealth, not for guns, planes, bombs, but for the health and welfare of our people—for free medical care for everyone, education and housing, guaranteed decent wages, and a clean environment for all. We cannot be secure by limiting our liberties, as some of our political leaders are demanding, but only by expanding them.

We should take our example not from our military and political leaders shouting "retaliate" and "war" but from the doctors and nurses and medical students and firemen and policemen who have been saving lives in the midst of mayhem, whose first thoughts are not vengeance but compassion, not violence but healing.

In the following pages we can find, from some of the most important thinkers across the centuries and around the globe, the historical and philosophical bases for opposition to war. Back in 1965, Beacon Press published *Instead of Violence: Writings by the Great Advocates of Peace and Nonviolence throughout History*. That volume traced pacifist thought back to Lao-tzu, writing in the sixth century before Christ, while the present book starts with the teachings of Buddha, in the same era. But while the progression of thought represented in the older volume necessarily ended with the 1960s, this one includes the thinking of writers and activists since that time, up to the first years of the new millennium.

While retaining some of the earlier essays by Ralph Waldo Emerson, Jane Addams, Scott Nearing, and Mohandas Gandhi, this volume carries new essays by Dorothy Day, Albert Camus, A. J. Muste, and Thomas Merton. It includes the historic speech made by Martin Luther King, Jr., at the Riverside Church in New York, when, against the advice of many of his associates, he spoke out boldly and eloquently against the war in Vietnam.

In the post-Vietnam period we hear from not only Western proponents of nonviolence—Daniel Berrigan, Jonathan Schell, Linus Pauling, and Tim Wise—but also from the Vietnamese spiritual leader Thich Nhat Hanh and the Japanese pacifist Daisaku Ikeda. With an essay by the brilliant Indian novelist Arundhati Roy, and an eloquent appeal by an international group of Nobel laureates, we challenge the latest American war, in Afghanistan.

The cry for peace in these essays is not simply a protest against war. It also presents a vision of a different world, and suggests a way to fulfill that vision. Against the makers of war, it proposes not passivity but resistance, a resistance that, because it is nonviolent, has a unique power greater than the power of guns and bombs.

I. Pre-Twentieth Century

Let a Man Overcome Anger by Love

(520 B.C.)

If a man by causing pain to others, wishes to obtain pleasure for himself, he, entangled in the bonds of sefishness, will never be free from hatred.

Let a man overcome anger by love, let him overcome evil by good; let him overcome the greedy by liberality, the liar by truth!

For hatred does not cease by hatred at any time; hatred ceases by love; this is an old rule.

Speak the truth; do not yield to anger; give, if thou art asked; by these three steps thou wilt become divine.

Let a wise man blow off the impurities of his self, as a smith blows off the impurities of silver, one by one, little by little, and from time to time.

Lead others, not by violence, but by law and equity.

He who possesses virtue and intelligence, who is just, speaks the truth, and does what is his own business, him the world will hold dear.

And the Blessed One observed the ways of society and noticed how much misery came from malignity and foolish offences done only to gratify vanity and self-seeking pride.

And Buddha said: "If a man foolishly does me wrong, I will return to him the protection of my ungrudging love; the more evil comes from

3

him, the more good shall go from me; the fragrance of goodness always comes to me, and the harmful air of evil goes to him."

A foolish man learning that Buddha observed the principle of great love which commends to return good for evil, came and abused him. Buddha was silent, pitying his folly.

The man having finished his abuse, Buddha asked him, saying: "Son, if a man declined to accept a present made to him, to whom would it belong?" And he answered: "In that case it would belong to the man who offered it."

"My son," said Buddha, "you have railed at me, but I decline to accept your abuse, and request you to keep it yourself. Will it not be a source of misery to you? As the echo belongs to the sound, and the shadow to the substance, so misery will overtake the evildoer without fail."

The abuser made no reply, and Buddha continued:

"A wicked man who reproaches a virtuous one is like one who looks up and spits at heaven; the spittle soils not the heaven, but comes back and defiles his own person.

"The slanderer is like one who flings dust at another when the wind is contrary; the dust does but return on him who threw it. The virtuous man cannot be hurt, and the misery that the other would inflict comes back on himself."

The abuser went away ashamed, but he came again and took refuge in the Buddha, the Dharma and the Sangha.

William Penn

from "Essay Towards the Present and Future Peace of Europe"

(1693)

As Justice is a Preserver, so it is a better Procurer of Peace than War. Though *Pax quoeritur bello* be a usual Saying, Peace is the end of War, and as such it was taken up by O.C. for his Motto. Yet the Use generally made of that expression shows us that properly and truly speaking, Men seek their Wills by War rather than Peace, and that as they will violate it to obtain them, so they will hardly be brought to think of Peace unless their Appetites be some Way gratified. If we look over the Stories of all Times, we shall find the Aggressors generally moved by Ambition; the Pride of Conquest and Greatness of Dominion more than Right. But as those Leviathans appear rarely in the World, so I shall anon endeavor to make it evident they had never been able to devour the Peace of the World, and engross whole Countries as they have done, if the Proposal I have to make for the Benefit of our present Age had been then in Practice. The Advantage that Justice has upon War is seen by the Success of Embassies, that so often prevent War by hearing the Pleas and Memorials of Justice in the Hands and Mouths of the Wronged Party. Perhaps it may be in a good Degree owing to Reputation or Poverty, or some Particular Interest or Conveniency of Princes and States, as much as Justice; but it is certain that as War cannot in any Sense be justified, but upon Wrongs received, and Right, upon Complaint, refused; so the Generality of Wars have their Rise from some such Pretension. This is better seen and understood at Home; for that which prevents a Civil War in a Nation is that which may prevent it Abroad, viz., Justice; and we see where that is notably obstructed, War is kindled between the Magistrates and People in particular Kingdoms and States; which, however it may be unlawful on the side of the People, we see never fails to follow, and ought to give the same Caution to Princes as if it were the Right of the People to do it: though I must needs say, the Remedy is almost ever worse than the Disease: the Aggressors seldom getting what they seek, or performing, if they prevail, what they promised: and the Blood and Poverty that usually attend the Enterprise, weigh more on Earth, as well as in Heaven, than what they lost or suffered, or what they get by endeavoring to mend their Condition, comes to: which Disappointment seems to be the Voice of Heaven, and Judgment of God against those violent Attempts. But to return, I say, Justice is the Means of Peace, betwixt the Government and the People, and one Man and Company and another. It prevents Strife, and at last ends it: for besides Shame or Fear, to contend longer, he or they being under Government, are constrained to bound their Desires and Resentment with the Satisfaction the Law gives. Thus Peace is maintained by Justice, which is a Fruit of Government, as Government is from Society, and Society from Consent.

There is another manifest Benefit which redounds to Christendom, by this Peaceable Expedient: the Reputation of Christianity will in some Degree be recovered in the Sight of Infidels; which, by the many Bloody and unjust Wars of Christians, not only with them, but one with another, hath been greatly impaired. For, to the Scandal of that Holy Profession, Christians that glory in their Saviour's Name have long devoted the Credit and Dignity of it, to their wordly Passions, as often as they have been excited by the Impulses of Ambition or Revenge. They have not always been in the Right: nor has Right been the Reason of War: and not only Christians against Christians but the same Sort of Christians have embrewed their Hands in one another's Blood: Invoking and Interesting, all they could, the Good and Merciful God to prosper their Arms to their Brethren's Destruction: yet their Saviour has told them that he came to save, and not to destroy the Lives of Men: to give and plant Peace among Men: and if in any Sense he may be said to send War, it is the Holy War indeed; for it is against the Devil, and not the Persons of Men. Of all his Titles this seems the most Glorious as well as comfortable for us, that he is the Prince of Peace. It is his Nature, his Office, his Work, and the End and excellent Blessing of his Coming, who is both the Maker and Preserver of our Peace with God. And it is very remarkable that in all the New Testament he is but once called Lion, but frequently the Lamb of God; and that those who desire to be the Disciples of his Cross and Kingdom, for they are inseparable, must be like him, as St. Paul, St. Peter and St. John tell us. Nor is it said the Lamb shall lie down with the Lion, but the Lion shall lie down with the Lamb. That is, War shall yield to Peace, and the Soldier turn Hermit. To be sure, Christians should not be apt to strive, not swift to Anger against anybody, and less with one another, and least of all for the uncertain and fading Enjoyments of this Lower World: and no Quality is exempted from this Doctrine. Here is a wide Field for the Reverend Clergy of Europe to act their Part in, who have so much the Possession of Princes and People too. May they recommend and labor this pacific Means I offer, which will end Blood, if not Strife; and then Reason, upon free Debate, will be Judge, and not the Sword. So that both Right and Peace, which are the Desire and Fruit of wise Governments, and the choice Blessings of any Country, seem to succeed the Establishment of this Proposal.

Ralph Waldo Emerson

from "War"

(1838)

That the project of peace should appear visionary to great numbers of sensible men; should appear laughable, even, to numbers; should appear to the grave and good-natured to be embarrassed with extreme practical difficulties, is very natural. "This is a poor, tedious society of yours," they say; "we do not see what good can come of it. Peace! Why, we are all at peace now. But if a foreign nation should wantonly insult or plunder our commerce, or, worse yet, should land on our shores to rob and kill, you would not have us sit, and be robbed and killed? You mistake the times; you overestimate the virtue of men. You forget that the quiet which now sleeps in cities and in farms, which lets the wagon go unguarded and the farmhouse unbolted, rests on the perfect understanding of all men that the musket, the halter and the jail stand behind there, ready to punish any disturber of it. All admit that this would be the best policy, if the world were all a church, if all men were the best men, if all would agree to accept this rule. But it is absurd for one nation to attempt it alone."

In the first place, we answer that we never make much account of objections which merely respect the actual state of the world at this moment, but which admit the general expediency and permanent excellence of the project. What is the best must be the true; and what is true— that is, what is at bottom fit and agreeable to the constitution of man—

must at last prevail over all obstruction and all opposition. There is no good now enjoyed by society that was not once as problematical and visionary as this. It is the tendency of the true interest of man to become his desire and steadfast aim.

But, further, it is a lesson which all history teaches wise men, to put trust in ideas, and not in circumstances. We have all grown up in the sight of frigates and navy yards, of armed forts and islands, of arsenals and militia. The reference to any foreign register will inform us of the number of thousand or million men that are now under arms in the vast colonial system of the British Empire, of Russia, Austria and France; and one is scared to find at what a cost the peace of the globe is kept. This vast apparatus of artillery, of fleets, of stone bastions and trenches and embankments; this incessant patrolling of sentinels; this waving of national flags; this reveille and evening gun; this martial music and endless playing of marches and singing of military and naval songs seem to us to constitute an imposing actual, which will not yield in centuries to the feeble, deprecatory voices of a handful of friends of peace.

Thus always we are daunted by the appearances; not seeing that their whole value lies at bottom in the state of mind. It is really a thought that built this portentous war establishment, and a thought shall also melt it away. Every nation and every man instantly surround themselves with a material apparatus which exactly corresponds to their moral state, or their state of thought. Observe how every truth and every error, each a *thought* of some man's mind, clothes itself with societies, houses, cities, language, ceremonies, newspapers. Observe the ideas of the present day—orthodoxy, skepticism, missions, popular education, temperance, anti-masonry, antislavery; see how each of these abstractions has embodied itself in an imposing apparatus in the community; and how timber, brick, lime and stone have flown into convenient shape, obedient to the master idea reigning in the minds of many persons.

You shall hear, someday, of a wild fancy which some man has in his brain, of the mischief of secret oaths. Come again one or two years afterwards, and you shall see it has built great houses of solid wood and brick and mortar. You shall see a hundred presses printing a million sheets; you shall see men and horses and wheels made to walk, run and roll for it: this great body of matter thus executing that one man's wild thought. This happens daily, yearly about us, with half thoughts, often with flimsy lies, pieces of policy and speculation. With good nursing they will last three or four years before they will come to nothing. But when a truth appears—as, for instance, a perception in the wit of one Columbus that there is land in the Western Sea; though he alone of all men has that thought, and they all jeer, it will build ships; it will build fleets; it will carry over half Spain and half England; it will plant a colony, a state, nations and half a globe full of men.

We surround ourselves always, according to our freedom and ability, with true images of ourselves in things, whether it be ships or books or cannon or churches. The standing army, the arsenal, the camp and the gibbet do not appertain to man. They only serve as an index to show where man is now; what a bad, ungoverned temper he has; what an ugly neighbor he is; how his affections halt; how low his hope lies. He who loves the bristle of bayonets only sees in their glitter what beforehand he feels in his heart. It is avarice and hatred; it is that quivering lip, that cold, hating eye, which built magazines and powder houses.

It follows of course that the least change in the man will change his circumstances; the least enlargement of his ideas, the least mitigation of his feelings in respect to other men; if, for example, he could be inspired with a tender kindness to the souls of men, and should come to feel that every man was another self with whom he might come to join, as left hand works with right. Every degree of the ascendancy of this feeling would cause the most striking changes of external things: the tents would be struck; the men-of-war would rot ashore; the arms rust; the cannon would become streetposts; the pikes, a fisher's harpoon; the marching regiment would be a caravan of emigrants, *peaceful* pioneers at the fountains of the Wabash and the Missouri. And so it must and will be: bayonet and sword must first retreat a little from their ostentatious prominence; then quite hide themselves, as the sheriff's halter does now, inviting the attendance only of relations and friends; and then, lastly, will be transferred to the museums of the curious, as poisoning and torturing tools are at this day.

War and peace thus resolve themselves into a mercury of the state of cultivation. At a certain stage of his progress, the man fights, if he be of a sound body and mind. At a certain higher stage he makes no offensive

Ralph Waldo Emerson

demonstration, but is alert to repel injury, and of an unconquerable heart. At a still higher stage he comes into the region of holiness; passion has passed away from him; his warlike nature is all converted into an active medicinal principle; he sacrifices himself, and accepts with alacrity wearisome tasks of denial and charity; but, being attacked, he bears it and turns the other cheek, as one engaged, throughout his being, no longer to the service of an individual but to the common soul of all men.

Since the peace question has been before the public mind, those who affirm its right and expediency have naturally been met with objections more or less weighty. There are cases frequently put by the curious— moral problems, like those problems in arithmetic which in long winter evenings the rustics try the hardness of their heads in ciphering out. And chiefly it is said, Either accept this principle for better, for worse, carry it out to the end, and meet its absurd consequences; or else, if you pretend to set an arbitrary limit, a "Thus far, no farther," then give up the principle, and take that limit which the common sense of all mankind has set, and which distinguishes offensive war as criminal, defensive war as just. Otherwise, if you go for no war, then be consistent, and give up self-defense in the highway, in your own house. Will you push it thus far? Will you stick to your principle of nonresistance when your strongbox is broken open, when your wife and babes are insulted and slaughtered in your sight? If you say yes, you only invite the robber and assassin; and a few bloody-minded desperadoes would soon butcher the good.

In reply to this charge of absurdity on the extreme peace doctrine, as shown in the supposed consequences, I wish to say that such deductions consider only one half of the fact. They look only at the passive side of the friend of peace, only at his passivity; they quite omit to consider his activity. But no man, it may be presumed, ever embraced the cause of peace and philanthropy for the sole end and satisfaction of being plundered and slain. A man does not come the length of the spirit of martyrdom without some active purpose, some equal motive, some flaming love. If you have a nation of men who have risen to that height of moral cultivation that they will not declare war or carry arms, for they have not so much madness left in their brains, you have a nation of lovers, of benefactors, of true, great and able men. Let me know more of that nation; I shall not find them defenseless, with idle hands springing at their sides. I shall find them men of love, honor and truth; men of an immense industry; men whose influence is felt to the end of the earth; men whose very look and voice carry the sentence of honor and shame; and all forces yield to their energy and persuasion. Whenever we see the doctrine of peace embraced by a nation, we may be assured it will not be one that invites injury; but one, on the contrary, which has a friend in the bottom of the heart of every man, even of the violent and the base; one against which no weapon can prosper; one which is looked upon as the asylum of the human race and has the tears and the blessings of mankind.

In the second place, as far as it respects individual action in difficult and extreme cases, I will say, such cases seldom or never occur to the good and just man; nor are we careful to say, or even to know, what in such crises is to be done. A wise man will never impawn his future being and action, and decide beforehand what he shall do in a given extreme event. Nature and God will instruct him in that hour.

The question naturally arises, How is this new aspiration of the human mind to be made visible and real? How is it to pass out of thoughts into things?

Not, certainly, in the first place, *in the way of routine and mere forms*— the universal specific of modern politics; not by organizing a society, and going through a course of resolutions and public manifestoes, and being thus formally accredited to the public and to the civility of the newspapers. We have played this game to tediousness. In some of our cities they choose noted duelists as presidents and officers of antidueling societies. Men who love that bloated vanity called public opinion think all is well if they have once got their bantling through a sufficient course of speeches and cheerings, of one, two or three public meetings; as if *they* could do anything: they vote and vote, cry hurrah on both sides, no man responsible, no man caring a pin. The next season, an Indian war, or an aggression on our commerce by Malays; or the party this man votes with have an appropriation to carry through Congress: instantly he wags his head the other way, and cries, Havoc and war!

This is not to be carried by public opinion, but by private opinion, by private conviction, by private, dear and earnest love. For the only hope of this cause is in the increased insight, and it is to be accomplished by the spontaneous teaching, of the cultivated soul, in its secret experience and meditation, that it is now time that it should pass out of the state of beast into the state of man; it is to hear the voice of God, which bids the devils that have rended and torn him come out of him and let him now be clothed and walk forth in his right mind.

Nor, in the next place, is the peace principle to be carried into effect by fear. It can never be defended, it can never be executed, by cowards. Everything great must be done in the spirit of greatness. The manhood that has been in war must be transferred to the cause of peace, before war can lose its charm, and peace be venerable to men....

The cause of peace is not the cause of cowardice. If peace is sought to be defended or preserved for the safety of the luxurious and the timid, it is a sham, and the peace will be base. War is better, and the peace will be broken. If peace is to be maintained, it must be by brave men, who have come up to the same height as the hero, namely, the will to carry their life in their hand, and stake it at any instant for their principle, but who have gone one step beyond the hero, and will not seek another man's life; men who have, by their intellectual insight or else by their moral elevation, attained such a perception of their own intrinsic worth that they do not think property or their own body a sufficient good to be saved by such dereliction of principle as treating a man like a sheep.

If the universal cry for reform of so many inveterate abuses, with which society rings; if the desire of a large class of young men for a faith and hope, intellectual and religious, such as they have not yet found, be an omen to be trusted; if the disposition to rely more in study and in action on the unexplored riches of the human constitution; if the search of the sublime laws of morals and the sources of hope and trust, in man, and not in books, in the present, and not in the past, proceed; if the rising generation can be provoked to think it unworthy to nestle into every abomination of the past, and shall feel the generous darings of austerity and virtue, then war has a short day, and human blood will cease to flow.

It is of little consequence in what manner, through what organs, this purpose of mercy and holiness is effected. The proposition of the congress of nations is undoubtedly that at which the present fabric of our society and the present course of events do point. But the mind, once prepared for the reign of principles, will easily find modes of expressing its will. There is the highest fitness in the place and time in which this enterprise is begun. Not in an obscure corner, not in a feudal Europe, not in an antiquated appanage where no onward step can be taken without rebellion, is this seed of benevolence laid in the furrow, with tears of hope; but in this broad America of God and man, where the forest is only now falling, or yet to fall, and the green earth opened to the inundation of emigrant men from all quarters of oppression and guilt; here, where not a family, not a few men, but mankind, shall say what shall be; here, we ask, Shall it be war, or shall it be peace?

Henry David Thoreau

Civil Disobedience

(1849)

I heartily accept the motto,—"That government is best which governs least;" and I should like to see it acted up to more rapidly and systematically. Carried out, it finally amounts to this, which also I believe,—"That government is best which governs not at all;" and when men are prepared for it, that will be the kind of government which they will have. Government is at best but an expedient; but most governments are usually, and all governments are sometimes, inexpedient. The objections which have been brought against a standing army, and they are many and weighty, and deserve to prevail, may also at last be brought against a standing government. The standing army is only an arm of the standing government. The government itself, which is only the mode which the people have chosen to execute their will, is equally liable to be abused and perverted before the people can act through it. Witness the present Mexican war, the work of comparatively a few individuals using the standing government as their tool; for, in the outset, the people would not have consented to this measure.

This American government,—what is it but a tradition, though a recent one, endeavoring to transmit itself unimpaired to posterity, but each instant losing some of its integrity? It has not the vitality and force of a single living man; for a single man can bend it to his will. It is a sort of wooden gun to the people themselves. But it is not the less necessary for this; for the people must have some complicated machinery or other, and hear its din, to satisfy that idea of government which they have. Governments show thus how successfully men can be imposed on, even impose on themselves, for their own advantage. It is excellent, we must all allow. Yet this government never of itself furthered any enterprise, but by the alacrity with which it got out of its way. *It* does not keep the country free. *It* does not settle the West. *It* does not educate. The character inherent in the American people has done all that has been accomplished; and it would have done somewhat more, if the government had not sometimes got in its way. For government is an expedient by which men would fain succeed in letting one another alone; and, as has been said, when it is most expedient, the governed are most let alone by it. Trade and commerce, if they were not made of India-rubber, would never manage to bounce over the obstacles which legislators are continually putting in their way; and, if one were to judge these men wholly by the effects of their actions and not partly by their intentions, they would deserve to be classed and punished with those mischievous persons who put obstructions on the railroads.

But, to speak practically and as a citizen, unlike those who call themselves no-government men, I ask for, not at once no government, but *at once* a better government. Let every man make known what kind of government would command his respect, and that will be one step toward obtaining it.

After all, the practical reason why, when the power is once in the hands of the people, a majority are permitted, and for a long period continue, to rule is not because they are most likely to be in the right, nor because this seems fairest to the minority, but because they are physically the strongest. But a government in which the majority rule in all cases cannot be based on justice, even as far as men understand it. Can there not be a government in which majorities do not virtually decide right and wrong, but conscience?—in which majorities decide only those questions to which the rule of expediency is applicable? Must the citizen ever for a moment, or in the least degree, resign his conscience to the legislator? Why has every man a conscience, then? I think that we should be men first, and subjects afterward. It is not desirable to cultivate a respect

Henry David Thoreau

for the law, so much as for the right. The only obligation which I have a right to assume is to do at any time what I think right. It is truly enough said, that a corporation has no conscience; but a corporation of conscientious men is a corporation *with* a conscience. Law never made men a whit more just; and, by means of their respect for it, even the well-disposed are daily made the agents of injustice. A common and natural result of an undue respect for law is, that you may see a file of soldiers, colonel, captain, corporal, privates, powder-monkeys, and all, marching in admirable order over hill and dale to the wars, against their wills, ay, against their common sense and consciences, which makes it very steep marching indeed, and produces a palpitation of the heart. They have no doubt that it is a damnable business in which they are concerned; they are all peaceably inclined. Now, what are they? Men at all? or small movable forts and magazines, at the service of some unscrupulous man in power? Visit the Navy-Yard, and behold a marine, such a man as an American government can make, or such as it can make a man with its black arts,—a mere shadow and reminiscence of humanity, a man laid out alive and standing, and already, as one may say, buried under arms with funeral accompaniments, though it may be,—

"Not a drum was heard, not a funeral note,
    As his corse to the rampart we hurried;
Not a soldier discharged his farewell shot
    O'er the grave where our hero we buried."

The mass of men serve the state thus, not as men mainly, but as machines, with their bodies. They are the standing army, and the militia, jailors, constables, posse comitatus, etc. In most cases there is no free exercise whatever of the judgment or of the moral sense; but they put themselves on a level with wood and earth and stones; and wooden men can perhaps be manufactured that will serve the purpose as well. Such command no more respect than men of straw or a lump of dirt. They have the same sort of worth only as horses and dogs. Yet such as these even are commonly esteemed good citizens. Others—as most legislators, politicians, lawyers, ministers, and office-holders—serve the state chiefly with their heads; and, as they rarely make any moral distinctions, they are as likely to serve the Devil, without *intending* it, as God. A very few, as heroes, patriots, martyrs, reformers in the great sense, and *men*, serve the state with their consciences also, and so necessarily resist it for the most part; and they are commonly treated as enemies by it. A wise man will only be useful as a man, and will not submit to be "clay," and "stop a hole to keep the wind away," but leave that office to his dust at least:—

"I am too high-born to be propertied,
To be a secondary at control,
Or useful serving-man and instrument
To any sovereign state throughout the world."

He who gives himself entirely to his fellow-men appears to them useless and selfish; but he who gives himself partially to them is pronounced a benefactor and philanthropist.

How does it become a man to behave toward this American government to-day? I answer, that he cannot without disgrace be associated with it. I cannot for an instant recognize that political organization as *my* government which is the *slave's* government also.

All men recognize the right of revolution; that is, the right to refuse allegiance to, and to resist, the government, when its tyranny or its inefficiency are great and unendurable. But almost all say that such is not the case now. But such was the case, they think, in the Revolution of '75. If one were to tell me that this was a bad government because it taxed certain foreign commodities brought to its ports, it is most probable that I should not make an ado about it, for I can do without them. All machines have their friction; and possibly this does enough good to counterbalance the evil. At any rate, it is a great evil to make a stir about it. But when the friction comes to have its machine, and oppression and robbery are organized, I say, let us not have such a machine any longer. In other words, when a sixth of the population of a nation which has undertaken to be the refuge of liberty are slaves, and a whole country is unjustly overrun and conquered by a foreign army, and subjected to military law, I think that it is not too soon for honest men to rebel and revolutionize. What makes this duty the more urgent is the fact that the country so overrun is not our own, but ours is the invading army.

Henry David Thoreau

Paley, a common authority with many on moral questions in his chapter on the "Duty of Submission to Civil Government," resolves all civil obligation into expediency; and he proceeds to say, "that so long as the interest of the whole society requires it, that is, so long as the established government cannot be resisted or changed without public inconveniency, it is the will of God that the established government be obeyed, and no longer.... This principle being admitted, the justice of every particular case of resistance is reduced to a computation of the quantity of the danger and grievance on the one side, and of the probability and expense of redressing it on the other." Of this, he says, every man shall judge for himself. But Paley appears never to have contemplated those cases to which the rule of expediency does not apply, in which a people, as well as an individual, must do justice, cost what it may. If I have unjustly wrested a plank from a drowning man, I must restore it to him though I drown myself. This, according to Paley, would be inconvenient. But he that would save his life, in such a case, shall lose it. This people must cease to hold slaves, and to make war on Mexico, though it cost them their existence as a people.

In their practice, nations agree with Paley; but does any one think that Massachusetts does exactly what is right at the present crisis?

> "A drab of state, a cloth-o'-silver slut,
> To have her train borne up, and her soul trail in the dirt."

Practically speaking, the opponents to a reform in Massachusetts are not a hundred thousand politicians at the South, but a hundred thousand merchants and farmers here, who are more interested in commerce and agriculture than they are in humanity, and are not prepared to do justice to the slave and to Mexico, *cost what it may.* I quarrel not with far-off foes, but with those who, near at home, coöperate with, and do the bidding of, those far away, and without whom the latter would be harmless. We are accustomed to say, that the mass of men are unprepared; but improvement is slow, because the few are not materially wiser or better than the many. It is not so important that many should be as good as you, as that there be some absolute goodness somewhere; for that will leaven the whole lump. There are thousands who are *in opinion* opposed to slavery and to the war, who yet in effect do nothing to put an end to them; who, esteeming themselves children of Washington and Franklin, sit down with their hands in their pockets, and say that they know not what to do, and do nothing; who even postpone the question of freedom to the question of free-trade, and quietly read the prices-current along with the latest advices from Mexico, after dinner, and, it may be, fall asleep over them both. What is the price-current of an honest man and patriot to-day? They hesitate, and they regret, and sometimes they petition; but they do nothing in earnest and with effect. They will wait, well disposed, for others to remedy the evil, that they may no longer have it to regret. At most, they give only a cheap vote, and a feeble countenance and God-speed, to the right, as it goes by them. There are nine hundred and ninety-nine patrons of virtue to one virtuous man. But it is easier to deal with the real possessor of a thing than with the temporary guardian of it.

All voting is a sort of gaming, like checkers or backgammon, with a slight moral tinge to it, a playing with right and wrong, with moral questions; and betting naturally accompanies it. The character of the voters is not staked. I cast my vote, perchance, as I think right; but I am not vitally concerned that that right should prevail. I am willing to leave it to the majority. Its obligation, therefore, never exceeds that of expediency. Even voting *for the right* is *doing* nothing for it. It is only expressing to men feebly your desire that it should prevail. A wise man will not leave the right to the mercy of chance, nor wish it to prevail through the power of the majority. There is but little virtue in the action of masses of men. When the majority shall at length vote for the abolition of slavery, it will be because they are indifferent to slavery, or because there is but little slavery left to be abolished by their vote. *They* will then be the only slaves. Only *his* vote can hasten the abolition of slavery who asserts his own freedom by his vote.

I hear of a convention to be held at Baltimore, or elsewhere, for the selection of a candidate for the Presidency, made up chiefly of editors, and men who are politicians by profession; but I think, what is it to any independent, intelligent, and respectable man what decision they may come to? Shall we not have the advantage of his wisdom and honesty, nevertheless? Can we not count upon some independent votes? Are there not many individuals in the country who do not attend conventions? But no:

Henry David Thoreau

I find that the respectable man, so called, has immediately drifted from his position, and despairs of his country, when his country has more reason to despair of him. He forthwith adopts one of the candidates thus selected as the only *available* one, thus proving that he is himself *available* for any purposes of the demagogue. His vote is of no more worth than that of any unprincipled foreigner or hireling native, who may have been bought. O for a man who is a *man*, and, as my neighbor says, has a bone in his back which you cannot pass your hand through! Our statistics are at fault: the population has been returned too large. How many *men* are there to a square thousand miles in this country? Hardly one. Does not America offer any inducement for men to settle here? The American has dwindled into an Odd Fellow,—one who may be known by the development of his organ of gregariousness, and a manifest lack of intellect and cheerful self-reliance; whose first and chief concern, on coming into the world, is to see that the Almshouses are in good repair; and, before yet he has lawfully donned the virile garb, to collect a fund for the support of the widows and orphans that may be; who, in short, ventures to live only by the aid of the Mutual Insurance company, which has promised to bury him decently.

It is not a man's duty, as a matter of course, to devote himself to the eradication of any, even the most enormous wrong; he may still properly have other concerns to engage him; but it is his duty, at least, to wash his hands of it, and, if he gives it no thought longer, not to give it practically his support. If I devote myself to other pursuits and contemplations, I must first see, at least, that I do not pursue them sitting upon another man's shoulders. I must get off him first, that he may pursue his contemplations too. See what gross inconsistency is tolerated. I have heard some of my townsmen say, "I should like to have them order me out to help put down an insurrection of the slaves, or to march to Mexico;—see if I would go;" and yet these very men have each, directly by their allegiance, and so indirectly, at least, by their money, furnished a substitute. The soldier is applauded who refuses to serve in an unjust war by those who do not refuse to sustain the unjust government which makes the war; is applauded by those whose own act and authority he disregards and sets at naught; as if the state were penitent to that degree that it hired one to scourge it while it sinned, but not to that degree that it left off sinning for a moment. Thus, under the name of Order and Civil Government, we are all made at last to pay homage to and support our own meanness. After the first blush of sin comes its indifference; and from immoral it becomes, as it were, *un*moral, and not quite unnecessary to that life which we have made.

The broadest and most prevalent error requires the most disinterested virtue to sustain it. The slight reproach to which the virtue of patriotism is commonly liable, the noble are most likely to incur. Those who, while they disapprove of the character and measures of a government, yield to it their allegiance and support are undoubtedly its most conscientious supporters, and so frequently the most serious obstacles to reform. Some are petitioning the state to dissolve the Union, to disregard the requisitions of the President. Why do they not dissolve it themselves,—the union between themselves and the state,—and refuse to pay their quota into its treasury? Do not they stand in the same relation to the state that the state does to the Union? And have not the same reasons prevented the state from resisting the Union which have prevented them from resisting the state?

How can a man be satisfied to entertain an opinion merely, and enjoy *it?* Is there any enjoyment in it, if his opinion is that he is aggrieved? If you are cheated out of a single dollar by your neighbor, you do not rest satisfied with knowing that you are cheated, or with saying that you are cheated, or even with petitioning him to pay you your due; but you take effectual steps at once to obtain the full amount, and see that you are never cheated again. Action from principle, the perception and the performance of right, changes things and relations; it is essentially revolutionary, and does not consist wholly with anything which was. It not only divides states and churches, it divides families; ay, it divides the *individual,* separating the diabolical in him from the divine.

Unjust laws exist: shall we be content to obey them, or shall we endeavor to amend them, and obey them until we have succeeded, or shall we transgress them at once? Men generally, under such a government as this, think that they ought to wait until they have persuaded the majority to alter them. They think that, if they should resist, the remedy would be worse than the evil. But it is the fault of the government itself that the remedy *is* worse than the evil. *It* makes it worse. Why is it not more apt to

Henry David Thoreau

anticipate and provide for reform? Why does it not cherish its wise minority? Why does it cry and resist before it is hurt? Why does it not encourage its citizens to be on the alert to point out its faults, and *do* better than it would have them? Why does it always crucify Christ, and excommunicate Copernicus and Luther, and pronounce Washington and Franklin rebels?

One would think, that a deliberate and practical denial of its authority was the only offense never contemplated by government; else, why has it not assigned its definite, its suitable and proportionate penalty? If a man who has no property refuses but once to earn nine shillings for the state, he is put in prison for a period unlimited by any law that I know, and determined only by the discretion of those who placed him there; but if he should steal ninety times nine shillings from the state, he is soon permitted to go at large again.

If the injustice is part of the necessary friction of the machine of government, let it go, let it go: perchance it will wear smooth,—certainly the machine will wear out. If the injustice has a spring, or a pulley, or a rope, or a crank, exclusively for itself, then perhaps you may consider whether the remedy will not be worse than the evil; but if it is of such a nature that it requires you to be the agent of injustice to another, then, I say, break the law. Let your life be a counter friction to stop the machine. What I have to do is to see, at any rate, that I do not lend myself to the wrong which I condemn.

As for adopting the ways which the state has provided for remedying the evil, I know not of such ways. They take too much time, and a man's life will be gone. I have other affairs to attend to. I came into this world, not chiefly to make this a good place to live in, but to live in it, be it good or bad. A man has not everything to do, but something; and because he cannot do *everything*, it is not necessary that he should do *something* wrong. It is not my business to be petitioning the Governor or the Legislature any more than it is theirs to petition me; and if they should not hear my petition, what should I do then? But in this case the state has provided no way: its very Constitution is the evil. This may seem to be harsh and stubborn and unconciliatory; but it is to treat with utmost kindness and consideration the only spirit that can appreciate or deserves it. So is all change for the better, like birth and death, which convulse the body.

I do not hesitate to say, that those who call themselves Abolitionists should at once effectually withdraw their support, both in person and property, from the government of Massachusetts and not wait till they constitute a majority of one, before they suffer the right to prevail through them. I think that it is enough if they have God on their side, without waiting for that other one. Moreover, any man more right than his neighbors constitutes a majority of one already.

I meet this American government, or its representative, the state government, directly, and face to face, once a year—no more—in the person of its tax-gatherer; this is the only mode in which a man situated as I am necessarily meets it; and it then says distinctly, Recognize me; and the simplest, most effectual, and, in the present posture of affairs, the indispensablest mode of treating with it on this head, of expressing your little satisfaction with and love for it, is to deny it then. My civil neighbor, the tax-gatherer, is the very man I have to deal with,—for it is, after all, with men and not with parchment that I quarrel,—and he has voluntarily chosen to be an agent of the government. How shall he ever know well what he is and does as an officer of the government, or as a man, until he is obliged to consider whether he shall treat me, his neighbor, for whom he has respect, as a neighbor and well-disposed man, or as a maniac and disturber of the peace, and see if he can get over this obstruction to his neighborliness without a ruder and more impetuous thought or speech corresponding with his action. I know this well, that if one thousand, if one hundred, if ten men whom I could name,—if ten *honest* men only,— ay, if *one* HONEST man, in this State of Massachusetts, *ceasing to hold slaves*, were actually to withdraw from this copartnership, and be locked up in the county jail therefor, it would be the abolition of slavery in America. For it matters not how small the beginning may seem to be: what is once well done is done forever. But we love better to talk about it: that we say is our mission. Reform keeps many scores of newspapers in its service, but not one man. If my esteemed neighbor, the State's ambassador, who will devote his days to the settlement of the question of human rights in the Council Chamber, instead of being threatened with the prisons of Carolina, were to sit down the prisoner of Massachusetts, that State which is so anxious to foist the sin of slavery upon her sister,—though at present she can discover only an act of inhospitality to be the ground of a

Henry David Thoreau

quarrel with her,—the Legislature would not wholly waive the subject the following winter.

Under a government which imprisons any unjustly, the true place for a just man is also a prison. The proper place to-day, the only place which Massachusetts has provided for her freer and less desponding spirits, is in her prisons, to be put out and locked out of the State by her own act, as they have already put themselves out by their principles. It is there that the fugitive slave, and the Mexican prisoner on parole, and the Indian come to plead the wrongs of his race should find them; on that separate, but more free and honorable ground, where the State places those who are not *with* her, but *against* her,—the only house in a slave State in which a free man can abide with honor. If any think that their influence would be lost there, and their voices no longer afflict the ear of the State, that they would not be as an enemy within its walls, they do not know by how much truth is stronger than error, nor how much more eloquently and effectively he can combat injustice who has experienced a little in his own person. Cast your whole vote, not a strip of paper merely, but your whole influence. A minority is powerless while it conforms to the majority; it is not even a minority then; but it is irresistible when it clogs by its whole weight. If the alternative is to keep all just men in prison, or give up war and slavery, the State will not hesitate which to choose. If a thousand men were not to pay their tax-bills this year, that would not be a violent and bloody measure, as it would be to pay them, and enable the State to commit violence and shed innocent blood. This is, in fact, the definition of a peaceable revolution, if any such is possible. If the tax-gatherer, or any other public officer, asks me, as one has done, "But what shall I do?" my answer is, "If you really wish to do anything, resign your office." When the subject has refused allegiance, and the officer has resigned his office, then the revolution is accomplished. But even suppose blood should flow. Is there not a sort of blood shed when the conscience is wounded? Through this wound a man's real manhood and immortality flow out, and he bleeds to an everlasting death. I see this blood flowing now.

I have contemplated the imprisonment of the offender, rather than the seizure of his goods,—though both will serve the same purpose,— because they who assert the purest right, and consequently are most dangerous to a corrupt State, commonly have not spent much time in accumulating property. To such the State renders comparatively small service, and a slight tax is wont to appear exorbitant, particularly if they are obliged to earn it by special labor with their hands. If there were one who lived wholly without the use of money, the State itself would hesitate to demand it of him. But the rich man—not to make any invidious comparison—is always sold to the institution which makes him rich. Absolutely speaking, the more money, the less virtue; for money comes between a man and his objects, and obtains them for him; and it was certainly no great virtue to obtain it. It puts to rest many questions which he would otherwise be taxed to answer; while the only new question which it puts is the hard but superfluous one, how to spend it. Thus his moral ground is taken from under his feet. The opportunities of living are diminished in proportion as what are called the "means" are increased. The best thing a man can do for his culture when he is rich is to endeavor to carry out those schemes which he entertained when he was poor. Christ answered the Herodians according to their condition. "Show me the tribute-money," said he;—and one took a penny out of his pocket;—if you use money which has the image of Cæsar on it and which he has made current and valuable, that is, *if you are men of the State,* and gladly enjoy the advantages of Cæsar's government, then pay him back some of his own when he demands it. "Render therefore to Cæsar that which is Cæsar's, and to God those things which are God's,"—leaving them no wiser than before as to which was which; for they did not wish to know.

When I converse with the freest of my neighbors, I perceive that, whatever they may say about the magnitude and seriousness of the question, and their regard for the public tranquillity, the long and the short of the matter is, that they cannot spare the protection of the existing government, and they dread the consequences to their property and families of disobedience to it. For my own part, I should not like to think that I ever rely on the protection of the State. But, if I deny the authority of the State when it presents its tax-bill, it will soon take and waste all my property, and so harass me and my children without end. This is hard. This makes it impossible for a man to live honestly, and at the same time comfortably, in outward respects. It will not be worth the while to accumulate property; that would be sure to go again. You must hire or squat somewhere, and raise but a small crop, and eat that soon. You must live within yourself, and depend upon yourself always tucked up and ready for a start, and not have many affairs. A man may grow rich in Turkey even, if he will be in all respects a good subject of the Turkish government. Confucius said: "If a state is governed by the principles of reason, poverty and misery are subjects of shame; if a state is not governed by the principles of reason, riches and honors are the subjects of shame." No: until I want the protection of Massachusetts to be extended to me in some distant Southern port, where my liberty is endangered, or until I am bent solely on building up an estate at home by peaceful enterprise, I can afford to refuse allegiance to Massachusetts, and her right to my property and life. It costs me less in every sense to incur the penalty of disobedience to the State than it would to obey. I should feel as if I were worth less in that case.

Some years ago, the State met me in behalf of the Church, and commanded me to pay a certain sum toward the support of a clergyman whose preaching my father attended, but never I myself. "Pay," it said, "or be locked up in the jail." I declined to pay. But, unfortunately, another man saw fit to pay it. I did not see why the schoolmaster should be taxed to support the priest, and not the priest the schoolmaster; for I was not the State's schoolmaster, but I supported myself by voluntary subscription. I did not see why the lyceum should not present its tax-bill, and have the State to back its demand, as well as the Church. However, at the request of the selectmen, I condescended to make some such statement as this in writing:—"Know all men by these presents, that I, Henry Thoreau, do not wish to be regarded as a member of any incorporated society which I have not joined." This I gave to the town clerk; and he has it. The State, having thus learned that I did not wish to be regarded as a member of that church, has never made a like demand on me since; though it said that it must adhere to its original presumption that time. If I had known how to name them, I should then have signed off in detail from all the societies which I never signed on to; but I did not know where to find a complete list.

I have paid no poll-tax for six years. I was put into a jail once on this account, for one night; and, as I stood considering the walls of solid stone, two or three feet thick, the door of wood and iron, a foot thick, and the iron grating which strained the light, I could not help being struck with the foolishness of that institution which treated me as if I were mere flesh and blood and bones, to be locked up. I wondered that it should have concluded at length that this was the best use it could put me to, and had never thought to avail itself of my services in some way. I saw that, if there was a wall of stone between me and my townsmen, there was a still more difficult one to climb or break through before they could get to be as free as I was. I did not for a moment feel confined, and the walls seemed a great waste of stone and mortar. I felt as if I alone of all my townsmen had paid my tax. They plainly did not know how to treat me, but behaved like persons who are underbred. In every threat and in every compliment there was a blunder; for they thought that my chief desire was to stand the other side of that stone wall. I could not but smile to see how industriously they locked the door on my meditations, which followed them out again without let or hindrance, and *they* were really all that was dangerous. As they could not reach me, they had resolved to punish my body; just as boys, if they cannot come at some person against whom they have a spite, will abuse his dog. I saw that the State was half-witted, that it was timid as a lone woman with her silver spoons, and that it did not know its friends from its foes, and I lost all my remaining respect for it, and pitied it.

Thus the State never intentionally confronts a man's sense, intellectual or moral, but only his body, his senses. It is not armed with superior wit or honesty, but with superior physical strength. I was not born to be forced. I will breathe after my own fashion. Let us see who is the strongest. What force has a multitude? They only can force me who obey a higher law than I. They force me to become like themselves. I do not hear of *men* being *forced* to live this way or that by masses of men. What sort of life were that to live? When I meet a government which says to me, "Your money or your life," why should I be in haste to give it my money? It may be in a great strait, and not know what to do: I cannot help that. It must help itself; do as I do. It is not worth the while to snivel about it. I am not responsible for the successful working of the machinery of society. I am not the son of the engineer. I perceive that, when an acorn and a chestnut fall side by side, the one does not remain inert to make way for the other, but both obey their own laws, and spring and grow and flourish as best they can, till one, perchance, overshadows and destroys the other. If a plant cannot live according to its nature, it dies; and so a man.

The night in prison was novel and interesting enough. The prisoners in their shirt-sleeves were enjoying a chat and the evening air in the doorway, when I entered. But the jailer said, "Come, boys, it is time to lock up;" and so they dispersed, and I heard the sound of their steps returning into the hollow apartments. My room-mate was introduced to me by the jailer as "a first-rate fellow and a clever man." When the door was locked, he showed me where to hang my hat, and how he managed matters there. The rooms were white-washed once a month; and this one, at least, was the whitest, most simply furnished, and probably the neatest apartment in the town. He naturally wanted to know where I came from, and what brought me there; and, when I had told him, I asked him in my turn how he came there, presuming him to be an honest man, of course; and, as the world goes, I believe he was. "Why," said he, "they accuse me of burning a barn; but I never did it." As near as I could discover, he had probably gone to bed in a barn when drunk, and smoked his pipe there; and so a barn was burnt. He had the reputation of being a clever man, had been there some three months waiting for his trial to come on, and would have to wait as much longer; but he was quite domesticated and contented, since he got his board for nothing, and thought that he was well treated.

He occupied one window, and I the other; and I saw that if one stayed there long, his principal business would be to look out the window. I had soon read all the tracts that were left there, and examined where former prisoners had broken out, and where a grate had been sawed off, and heard the history of the various occupants of that room; for I found that even here there was a history and a gossip which never circulated beyond the walls of the jail. Probably this is the only house in the town where verses are composed, which are afterward printed in a circular form, but not published. I was shown quite a long list of verses which were composed by some young men who had been detected in an attempt to escape, who avenged themselves by singing them.

I pumped my fellow-prisoner as dry as I could, for fear I should never see him again; but at length he showed me which was my bed, and left me to blow out the lamp.

It was like traveling into a far country, such as I had never expected to behold, to lie there for one night. It seemed to me that I never had heard the town-clock strike before, nor the evening sounds of the village; for we slept with the windows open, which were inside the grating. It was to see my native village in the light of the Middle Ages, and our Concord was turned into a Rhine stream, and visions of knights and castles passed before me. They were the voices of old burghers that I heard in the streets. I was an involuntary spectator and auditor of whatever was done and said in the kitchen of the adjacent village-inn,—a wholly new and rare experience to me. It was a closer view of my native town. I was fairly inside of it. I never had seen its institutions before. This is one of its peculiar institutions; for it is a shire town. I began to comprehend what its inhabitants were about.

In the morning, our breakfasts were put through the hole in the door, in small oblong-square tin pans, made to fit, and holding a pint of chocolate, with brown bread, and an iron spoon. When they called for the vessels again, I was green enough to return what bread I had left; but my comrade seized it, and said that I should lay that up for lunch or dinner. Soon after he was let out to work at haying in a neighboring field, whither he went every day, and would not be back till noon; so he bade me good-day, saying that he doubted if he should see me again.

When I came out of prison,—for some one interfered, and paid that tax,—I did not perceive that great changes had taken place on the common, such as he observed who went in a youth and emerged a tottering and gray-headed man; and yet a change had to my eyes come over the scene,—the town, and State, and country,—greater than any that mere time could effect. I saw yet more distinctly the State in which I lived. I saw to what extent the people among whom I lived could be trusted as good neighbors and friends; that their friendship was for summer weather only; that they did not greatly propose to do right; that they were a distinct race from me by their prejudices and superstitions, as the Chinamen and Malays are; that in their sacrifices to humanity they ran no risks, not even to their property; that after all they were not so noble but they treated the thief as he had treated them, and hoped, by a certain outward observance and a few prayers, and by walking in a particular straight though useless path from time to time, to save their souls. This

Henry David Thoreau

may be to judge my neighbors harshly; for I believe that many of them are not aware that they have such an institution as the jail in their village.

It was formerly the custom in our village, when a poor debtor came out of jail, for his acquaintances to salute him, looking through their fingers, which were crossed to represent the grating of a jail window, "How do ye do?" My neighbors did not thus salute me, but first looked at me, and then at one another, as if I had returned from a long journey. I was put into jail as I was going to the shoemaker's to get a shoe which was mended. When I was let out the next morning, I proceeded to finish my errand, and, having put on my mended shoe, joined a huckleberry party, who were impatient to put themselves under my conduct; and in half an hour,—for the horse was soon tackled,—was in the midst of a huckleberry field, on one of our highest hills, two miles off, and then the State was nowhere to be seen.

This is the whole history of "My Prisons."

I have never declined paying the highway tax, because I am as desirous of being a good neighbor as I am of being a bad subject; and as for supporting schools, I am doing my part to educate my fellow-countrymen now. It is for no particular item in the tax-bill that I refuse to pay it. I simply wish to refuse allegiance to the State, to withdraw and stand aloof from it effectually. I do not care to trace the course of my dollar, if I could, till it buys a man or a musket to shoot with,—the dollar is innocent,—but I am concerned to trace the effects of my allegiance. In fact, I quietly declare war with the State, after my fashion, though I will still make what use and get what advantage of her I can, as is usual in such cases.

If others pay the tax which is demanded of me, from a sympathy with the State, they do but what they have already done in their own case, or rather they abet injustice to a greater extent than the State requires. If they pay the tax from a mistaken interest in the individual taxed, to save his property, or prevent his going to jail, it is because they have not considered wisely how far they let their private feelings interfere with the public good.

This, then, is my position at present. But one cannot be too much on his guard in such a case, lest his action be biased by obstinacy or an undue regard for the opinions of men. Let him see that he does only what belongs to himself and to the hour.

I think sometimes, Why, this people mean well, they are only ignorant; they would do better if they knew how: why give your neighbors this pain to treat you as they are not inclined to? But I think again, This is no reason why I should do as they do, or permit others to suffer much greater pain of a different kind. Again, I sometimes say to myself, When many millions of men, without heat, without ill will, without personal feeling of any kind, demand of you a few shillings only, without the possibility, such is their constitution, of retracting or altering their present demand, and without the possibility, on your side, of appeal to any other millions, why expose yourself to this overwhelming brute force? You do not resist cold and hunger, the winds and the waves, thus obstinately; you quietly submit to a thousand similar necessities. You do not put your head into the fire. But just in proportion as I regard this as not wholly a brute force, but partly a human force, and consider that I have relations to those millions as to so many millions of men, and not of mere brute or inanimate things, I see that appeal is possible, first and instantaneously, from them to the Maker of them, and, secondly, from them to themselves. But if I put my head deliberately into the fire, there is no appeal to fire or to the Maker of fire, and I have only myself to blame. If I could convince myself that I have any right to be satisfied with men as they are, and to treat them accordingly, and not according, in some respects, to my requisitions and expectations of what they and I ought to be, then, like a good Mussulman and fatalist, I should endeavor to be satisfied with things as they are, and say it is the will of God. And, above all, there is this difference between resisting this and a purely brute or natural force, that I can resist this with some effect; but I cannot expect, like Orpheus, to change the nature of the rocks and trees and beasts.

I do not wish to quarrel with any man or nation. I do not wish to split hairs, to make fine distinctions, or set myself up as better than my neighbors. I seek rather, I may say, even an excuse for conforming to the laws of the land. I am but too ready to conform to them. Indeed, I have reason to suspect myself on this head; and each year, as the tax-gatherer comes round, I find myself disposed to review the acts and position of the general and State governments, and the spirit of the people, to discover a pretext for conformity.

Henry David Thoreau

"We must affect our country as our parents,
And if at any time we alienate
Our love or industry from doing it honor,
We must respect effects and teach the soul
Matter of conscience and religion,
And not desire of rule or benefit."

I believe that the State will soon be able to take all my work of this sort out of my hands, and then I shall be no better a patriot than my fellow-countrymen. Seen from a lower point of view, the Constitution, with all its faults, is very good; the law and the courts are very respectable; even this State and this American government are, in many respects, very admirable, and rare things, to be thankful for, such as a great many have described them; but seen from a point of view a little higher, they are what I have described them; seen from a higher still, and the highest, who shall say what they are, or that they are worth looking at or thinking of at all?

However, the government does not concern me much, and I shall bestow the fewest possible thoughts on it. It is not many moments that I live under a government, even in this world. If a man is thought-free, fancy-free, imagination-free, that which *is not* never for a long time appearing *to be* to him, unwise rulers or reformers cannot fatally interrupt him.

I know that most men think differently from myself; but those whose lives are by profession devoted to the study of these or kindred subjects content me as little as any. Statesmen and legislators, standing so completely within the institution, never distinctly and nakedly behold it. They speak of moving society, but have no resting-place without it. They may be men of a certain experience and discrimination, and have no doubt invented ingenious and even useful systems, for which we sincerely thank them; but all their wit and usefulness lie within certain not very wide limits. They are wont to forget that the world is not governed by policy and expediency. Webster never goes behind government, and so cannot speak with authority about it. His words are wisdom to those legislators who contemplate no essential reform in the existing government; but for thinkers, and those who legislate for all time, he never once glances at the subject. I know of those whose serene and wise speculations on this theme would soon reveal the limits of his mind's range and hospitality. Yet, compared with the cheap professions of most reformers, and the still cheaper wisdom and eloquence of politicians in general, his are almost the only sensible and valuable words, and we thank Heaven for him. Comparatively, he is always strong, original, and, above all, practical. Still, his quality is not wisdom, but prudence. The lawyer's truth is not Truth, but consistency or a consistent expediency. Truth is always in harmony with herself, and is not concerned chiefly to reveal the justice that may consist with wrong-doing. He well deserves to be called, as he has been called, the Defender of the Constitution. There are really no blows to be given by him but defensive ones. He is not a leader, but a follower. His leaders are the men of '87. "I have never made an effort," he says, "and never propose to make an effort; I have never countenanced an effort, and never mean to countenance an effort, to disturb the arrangement as originally made, by which the various States came into the Union." Still thinking of the sanction which the Constitution gives to slavery, he says, "Because it was a part of the original compact,—let it stand." Notwithstanding his special acuteness and ability, he is unable to take a fact out of its merely political relations, and behold it as it lies absolutely to be disposed of by the intellect,—what, for instance, it behooves a man to do here in America to-day with regard to slavery,—but ventures, or is driven, to make some such desperate answer as the following, while professing to speak absolutely, and as a private man,—from which what new and singular code of social duties might be inferred? "The manner," says he, "in which the governments of those States where slavery exists are to regulate it is for their own consideration, under their responsibility to their constituents, to the general laws of propriety, humanity, and justice, and to God. Associations formed elsewhere, springing from a feeling of humanity, or other cause, have nothing whatever to do with it. They have never received any encouragement from me, and they never will."

They who know of no purer sources of truth, who have traced up its stream no higher, stand, and wisely stand, by the Bible and the Constitution, and drink at it there with reverence and humility; but they who behold where it comes trickling into this lake or that pool, gird up their loins once more, and continue their pilgrimage toward its fountainhead.

No man with a genius for legislation has appeared in America. They are rare in the history of the world. There are orators, politicians, and eloquent men, by the thousand; but the speaker has not yet opened his mouth to speak who is capable of settling the much-vexed questions of the day. We love eloquence for its own sake, and not for any truth which it may utter, or any heroism it may inspire. Our legislators have not yet learned the comparative value of free-trade and of freedom, of union, and of rectitude, to a nation. They have no genius or talent for comparatively humble questions of taxation and finance, commerce and manufactures and agriculture. If we were left solely to the wordy wit of legislators in Congress for our guidance, uncorrected by the seasonable experience and the effectual complaints of the people, America would not long retain her rank among the nations. For eighteen hundred years, though perchance I have no right to say it, the New Testament has been written; yet where is the legislator who has wisdom and practical talent enough to avail himself of the light which it sheds on the science of legislation?

The authority of government, even such as I am willing to submit to,—for I will cheerfully obey those who know and can do better than I, and in many things even those who neither know nor can do so well,—is still an impure one: to be strictly just, it must have the sanction and consent of the governed. It can have no pure right over my person and property but what I concede to it. The progress from an absolute to a limited monarchy, from a limited monarchy to a democracy, is a progress toward a true respect for the individual. Even the Chinese philosopher was wise enough to regard the individual as the basis of the empire. Is a democracy, such as we know it, the last improvement possible in government? Is it not possible to take a step further towards recognizing and organizing the rights of man? There will never be a really free and enlightened State until the State comes to recognize the individual as a higher and independent power, from which all its own power and authority are derived, and treats him accordingly. I please myself with imagining a State at last which can afford to be just to all men, and to treat the individual with respect as a neighbor; which even would not think it inconsistent with its own repose if a few were to live aloof from it, not meddling with it, nor embraced by it, who fulfilled all the duties of neighbors and fellow-men. A State which bore this kind of fruit, and suffered it to drop off as fast as it ripened, would prepare the way for a still more perfect and glorious State, which also I have imagined, but not yet anywhere seen.

Henry David Thoreau

II. The Fin de Siècle to the Cold War
(1900–1949)

Jane Addams

from "Newer Ideals of Peace"

(1907)

It is quite possible that we have committed the time-honored folly of looking for a sudden change in men's attitude toward war, even as the poor alchemists wasted their lives in searching for a magic fluid and did nothing to discover the great laws governing chemical changes and reactions, the knowledge of which would have developed untold wealth beyond their crude dreams of transmuted gold.

The final moral reaction may at last come, accompanied by deep remorse, too tardy to reclaim all the human life which has been spent and the treasure which has been wasted, or it may come with a great sense of joy that all voluntary destruction of human life, all the deliberate wasting of the fruits of labor, have become a thing of the past, and that whatever the future contains for us, it will at least be free from war. We may at last comprehend the truth of that which Ruskin has stated so many times, that we worship the soldier not because he goes forth to slay, but to be slain.

That this world peace movement should be arising from the humblest without the sanction and in some cases with the explicit indifference, of the church founded by the Prince of Peace, is simply another example of the strange paths of moral evolution.

To some of us it seems clear that marked manifestations of this movement are found in the immigrant quarters of American cities. The previous survey of the immigrant situation would indicate that all the peoples of the world have become part of the American tribunal, and that their sense of pity, their clamor for personal kindness, their insistence upon the right to join in our progress, can no longer be disregarded. The burdens and sorrows of men have unexpectedly become intelligent and urgent to this nation, and it is only by accepting them with some magnanimity that we can develop the larger sense of justice which is becoming world-wide and is lying in ambush, as it were, to manifest itself in governmental relations. Men of all nations are determining upon the abolition of degrading poverty, disease and intellectual weakness, with their resulting industrial inefficiency, and are making a determined effort to conserve even the feeblest citizen to the state. To join in this determined effort is to break through national bonds and to unlock the latent fellowship between man and man. In a political campaign men will go through every possible hardship in response to certain political loyalties; in a moment of national danger men will sacrifice every personal advantage. It is but necessary to make this fellowship wider, to extend its scope without lowering its intensity. Those emotions which stir the spirit to deeds of self-surrender and to high enthusiasm, are among the world's most precious assets. That this emotion has so often become associated with war by no means proves that it cannot be used for other ends. There is something active and tangible in this new internationalism, although it is difficult to make it clear, and in our striving for a new word with which to express this new and important sentiment, we are driven to the rather absurd phrase of "cosmic patriotism." Whatever it may be called, it may yet be strong enough to move masses of men out of their narrow national considerations and cautions into new reaches of human effort and affection. Religion has long ago taught that only as the individual can establish a sense of union with a power for righteousness not himself can he experience peace; and it may be possible that the nations will be called to a similar experience.

The International Peace Conference held in Boston in 1904 was opened by a huge meeting in which men of influence and modern thought from four continents gave reasons for their belief in the passing of war. But none was so modern, so fundamental and so trenchant as the address which was read from the prophet Isaiah. He founded the cause of peace upon the cause of righteousness, not only as expressed in political relations, but also in industrial relations. He contended that peace could be secured only as men abstained from the gains of oppression and responded to the cause of the poor; that swords would finally be beaten into plowshares and pruning hooks, not because men resolved to be peaceful, but because all the metal of the earth would be turned to its proper use when the poor and their children should be abundantly fed. It was as if the ancient prophet foresaw that under an enlightened industrialism peace would no longer be an absence of war, but the unfolding of world-wide processes making for the nurture of human life. He predicted the moment which has come to us now that peace is no longer an abstract dogma but has become a rising tide of moral enthusiasm slowly engulfing all pride of conquest and making war impossible.

from *The Trial of Scott Nearing and the American Socialist Society*

(1919)

I told the District Attorney on the stand that I was opposed to all wars. I regard war as a social disease, something that afflicts society, that curses people. I do not suppose three people in a hundred like war. I do not suppose that three people in a hundred want war. There are some people who are pugnacious, and who love to fight, for the sake of a fight, and they might like war, but I do not believe there are three people in a hundred, certainly not five in a hundred, that do.

I believe the great majority of people agree with me that war is a curse, an unmitigated curse. All the things that come out of war come out in spite of war and not because of it.

The democracy that has come into Europe, whatever it is called, has come in spite of the war and not because of it. That would have come out in any case, and we would have had it without the expenditure of twenty million lives and a hundred and eighty billions of wealth.

I regard war as a social disease, a social curse, and I believe that we should stamp war out. To my mind the great curse of war is not that people are killed and injured, not that property is destroyed. That happens every day in peace times as well as in war times. To my mind the great curse of war is that it is built on fear and hate.

Now, fear and hate are primitive passions; the savages in the woods are intimidated by fear and hate. They do not belong in civilized society. In civilized society, for fear and hate we substitute constructive purposes and love. It is their positive virtues. When we fear things, we draw back from them. When we hate things, we want to destroy them.

In civilized society, instead of drawing away from things, and wanting to destroy them, we want to pull things together and build them up. Fear and hate are negatives. Peace and love are positives, and form the forces upon which civilization is built. And where we have collectively fear and hate, it is a means of menace to the order of the world.

Furthermore, during war, we ask people to go out and deliberately injure their fellows. We ask a man to go out and maim or kill another man against whom he has not a solitary thing in the world—a man who may be a good farmer, a good husband, a good son, and a good worker, and a good citizen. Another man comes out and shoots him down; that is, he goes out and raises his hand against his neighbor to do his neighbor damage. That is the way society is destroyed. Whenever you go out to pull things to pieces, whenever you go out to injure anybody, you are going out to destroy society. Society can never be built up unless you go out to help your neighbors.

The principle "each for all and all for each" is the fundamental social principle. People must work together if they are going to get anywhere. War teaches people to go out and destroy other people and to destroy other people's property.

And when Sherman said that war was hell, I believe that he meant, or at least to me that means, that war creates a hell inside of a man who goes to war. He is going to work himself up into a passion of hatred against somebody else, and that is hell.

The destruction of life and property is incidental. The destructive forces that that puts into a man's soul are fundamental. That is why I am opposed to all wars, just as I am opposed to all violence. I don't believe in any man having the right to go out and use violence against another man. That is not the right of one human being to have against the other, that is not the way you get brotherhood. That is the reason I told the District Attorney on the stand that I was against all wars. I am against dueling; I am against all violence of man against man, and war is one of those methods of violence.

I believe war is barbaric, I believe it is primitive, I believe it is a relic of a bygone age; I believe that society will be destroyed if built up that way. That is, I believe that they that take the sword must perish by the sword; just as they that set out to assist their neighbors are bound to build up a strong, cohesive, united society. That is the field over which I went in my direct testimony and in the cross-examination.

I have been a student of public affairs. I am a Socialist. I am a pacifist. But I am not charged with any of these things as offenses. On the other hand I believe that as an American citizen I have a right to discuss public questions. I think the judge will charge you so. I have a right to oppose the passage of a law. I think the judge will charge you so. I have a right under the law, after the law is passed, to agitate for a development of public sentiment that will result in a repeal of that law. I think the judge will charge you so.

In other words, as I said in the beginning, in a democracy, if we are to have a democracy, as a student of public affairs and as a Socialist and as a pacifist, I have a right to express my opinions. I may be wrong, utterly wrong, and nobody listen to me, nobody pay any attention to me. I have a right to express my opinions.

Gentlemen, I have been throughout my life as consistent as I could be. I have spoken and written for years, honestly and frankly. I went on the stand and I spoke to you as honestly as I know how. I answered the District Attorney's questions as honestly and as frankly as I could. I stand before you today as an advocate of economic justice and world brotherhood, and peace among all men.

Mohandas K. Gandhi

My Faith in Nonviolence

(1930)

I have found that life persists in the midst of destruction and, therefore, there must be a higher law than that of destruction. Only under that law would a well-ordered society be intelligible and life worth living. And if that is the law of life, we have to work it out in daily life. Wherever there are jars, wherever you are confronted with an opponent, conquer him with love. In a crude manner I have worked it out in my life. That does not mean that all my difficulties are solved. I have found, however, that this law of love has answered as the law of destruction has never done. In India we have had an ocular demonstration of the operation of this law on the widest scale possible. I do not claim therefore that nonviolence has necessarily penetrated the three hundred millions, but I do claim that it has penetrated deeper than any other message, and in an incredibly short time. We have not been all uniformly nonviolent; and with the vast majority, nonviolence has been a matter of policy. Even so, I want you to find out if the country has not made phenomenal progress under the protecting power of nonviolence.

It takes a fairly strenuous course of training to attain to a mental state of nonviolence. In daily life it has to be a course of discipline, though one may not like it—like, for instance, the life of a soldier. But I agree that, unless there is a hearty cooperation of the mind, the mere outward observance will be simply a mask, harmful both to the man himself and to others. The perfect state is reached only when mind and body and speech are in proper coordination. But it is always a case of intense mental struggle. It is not that I am incapable of anger, for instance, but I succeed on almost all occasions to keep my feelings under control. Whatever may be the result, there is always in me a conscious struggle for following the law of nonviolence deliberately and ceaselessly. Such a struggle leaves one stronger for it. Nonviolence is a weapon of the strong. With the weak it might easily be hypocrisy. Fear and love are contradictory terms. Love is reckless in giving away, oblivious as to what it gets in return. Love wrestles with the world as with the self and ultimately gains a mastery over all other feelings. My daily experience, as of those who are working with me, is that every problem lends itself to solution if we are determined to make the law of truth and nonviolence the law of life. For truth and nonviolence are, to me, faces of the same coin.

The law of love will work, just as the law of gravitation will work, whether we accept it or not. Just as a scientist will work wonders out of various applications of the law of nature, even so a man who applies the law of love with scientific precision can work greater wonders. For the force of nonviolence is infinitely more wonderful and subtle than the material forces of nature, like, for instance, electricity. The men who discovered for us the law of love were greater scientists than any of our modern scientists. Only our explorations have not gone far enough and so it is not possible for everyone to see all its workings. Such, at any rate, is the hallucination, if it is one, under which I am laboring. The more I work at this law the more I feel the delight in life, the delight in the scheme of this universe. It gives me a peace and a meaning of the mysteries of nature that I have no power to describe.

Mohandas K. Gandhi

Pacifism

(1936)

The Catholic Worker is sincerely a *pacifist* paper.

We oppose class war and class hatred, even while we stand opposed to injustice and greed. Our fight is not "with flesh and blood but principalities and powers."

We oppose also imperialist war.

We oppose, moreover, preparedness for war, a preparedness which is going on now on an unprecedented scale and which will undoubtedly lead to war. The Holy Father Pope Pius XI said, in a pastoral letter in 1929:

"And since the unbridled race for armaments is on the one hand the effect of the rivalry among nations and on the other cause of the withdrawal of enormous sums from the public wealth and hence not the smallest of contributors to the current extraordinary crisis. We cannot refrain from renewing on this subject the wise admonitions of our predecessors which thus far have not been heard.

"We exhort you all, Venerable Brethren, that by all the means at your disposal, both by preaching and by the press, you seek to illumine minds and open hearts on this matter, according to the solid dictates of right reason and of the Christian law."

"Why not prepare for peace?"

1. Let us think now what it means to be neutral in fact as well as in name.
2. American bankers must not lend money to nations at war.
3. We must renounce neutral rights at sea.

These three points are made by Herbert Agar in "Land of the Free." Neutrality "in fact," he says, could be practiced on by either saint or cynic.

In fact, it would mean that either we must not pass judgments (upholding a positive stand for peace instead) or else in condemning Italy, also to condemn Ethiopia for resisting. To do this one would indeed have to be either saint or cynic.

The cynic would say, "It is none of my business."

The Saint would say, and perhaps he would be a very wise man in saying it, "The conquered conquers in the end. Christ was overcome and He overcame. There was His ostensible failure on the Cross, yet He rose triumphant and Christianity spread over the world. The Christian thing to do would be not to resist, but when anyone asked for one's coat, to give up one's cloak besides." As Peter Maurin pointed out in the last instance, Australia could be given up to Japanese expansion for instance, if England objected on "noble" grounds for Japan's aggression in Manchuria. But recognizing that the majority of people are not Saints; that they are swift to wrath, to resist aggression (when they are not the aggressors), then we can only insist ceaselessly that even when the people are taking sides mentally they must keep out, they must not participate in "a War to end War."

In the last war we helped to impose an unjust peace, even if we grant that we sincerely thought we were engaged in a noble crusade and were throwing our support on the right side in the conflict. We were influenced to this way of thinking not only by deliberate propaganda, but also by the muddle-headedness of pacifists who were not truly "peace-lovers."

Example Again

If we are calling upon nations to disarm, we must be brave enough and courageous enough to set the example.

Nations can live at home. That is the title of a recent book, and many surveys are being made at present to find out how many nations can do without trade and "live at home."

If we abandoned our neutral rights at sea, we would still have a surplus of food and material goods with which to help feed nations which had been made gaunt by war. We are not suggesting this as a business note but as a reminder of Christian Charity.

Do we believe we help any country by participating in an evil in which they are engaged? We rather help them by maintaining our own peace. It takes a man of heroic stature to be a pacifist and we urge our readers to consider and study pacifism and disarmament in this light. A pacifist who is willing to endure the scorn of the unthinking mob, the ignominy of jail, the pain of stripes and the threat of death, cannot be lightly dismissed as a coward afraid of physical pain.

A pacifist even now must be prepared for the opposition of the next mob who thinks violence is bravery. The pacifist in the next war must be ready for martyrdom.

We call upon youth to prepare!

Our Country Passes from Undeclared War to Declared War; We Continue Our Christian Pacifist Stand

(1942)

Dear fellow workers in Christ:

Lord God, merciful God, our Father, shall we keep silent, or shall we speak? And if we speak, what shall we say?

I am sitting here in the church on Mott Street writing this in your presence. Out on the streets it is quiet, but you are there too, in the Chinese, in the Italians, these neighbors we love. We love them because they are our brothers, as Christ is our Brother and God our Father.

But we have forgotten so much. We have all forgotten. And how can we know unless you tell us. "For whoever calls upon the name of the Lord shall be saved." How then are they to call upon Him in whom they have not believed? But how are they to believe Him whom they have not heard? And how are they to hear, if no one preaches? And how are men to preach unless they be sent? As it is written, "How beautiful are the feet of those who preach the gospel of peace." (Romans X)

Seventy-five thousand Catholic Workers go out every month. What shall we print? We can print still what the Holy Father is saying, when he speaks of total war, of mitigating the horrors of war, when he speaks of cities of refuge, of feeding Europe....

We will print the words of Christ who is with us always, even to the end of the world. "Love your enemies, do good to those who hate you, and pray for those who persecute and calumniate you, so that you may be children of your Father in heaven, who makes His sun to rise on the good and the evil, and sends rain on the just and unjust."

We are at war, a declared war, with Japan, Germany and Italy. But still we can repeat Christ's words, each day, holding them close in our hearts, each month printing them in the paper. In times past, Europe has been a battlefield. But let us remember St. Francis, who spoke of peace and we will remind our readers of him, too, so they will not forget.

In The Catholic Worker we will quote our Pope, our saints, our priests. We will go on printing the articles which remind us today that we are all "called to be saints," that we are other Christs, reminding us of the priesthood of the laity.

We are still pacifists. Our manifesto is the Sermon on the Mount, which means that we will try to be peacemakers. Speaking for many of our conscientious objectors, we will not participate in armed warfare or in making munitions, or by buying government bonds to prosecute the war, or in urging others to these efforts.

But neither will we be carping in our criticism. We love our country and we love our President. We have been the only country in the world where men of all nations have taken refuge from oppression. We recognize that while in the order of intention we have tried to stand for peace, for love of our brother, in the order of execution we have failed as Americans in living up to our principles.

We will try daily, hourly, to pray for an end to the war, such an end, to quote Father Orchard, "as would manifest to all the world, that it was brought about by divine action, rather than by military might or diplomatic negotiation, which men and nations would then only attribute to their power or sagacity."

"Despite all calls to prayer," Father Orchard concludes, "there is at present all too little indication anywhere that the tragedy of humanity and the desperate need of the world have moved the faithful, still less stirred the thoughtless masses, to turn to prayer as the only hope for mankind this dreadful hour.

"We shall never pray until we feel more deeply, and we shall never feel deeply enough until we envisage what is actually happening in the world, and understand what is possible in the will of God; and that means until sufficient numbers realize that we have brought things to a pass which is beyond human power to help or save.

"Those who do feel and see, however inadequately, should not hesitate to begin to pray, or fail to persevere, however dark the prospects remain. Let them urge others to do likewise; and then, first small groups, and then the Church as a whole, and at last the world, may turn and cry for forgiveness, mercy and deliverance for all.

"Then we may be sure God will answer, and effectually; for the Lord's hand is not shortened that it cannot save, nor His ear heavy that it cannot hear." Let us add, that unless we combine this prayer with almsgiving, in giving to the least of God's children, and fasting in order that we may help feed the hungry, and penance in recognition of our share in the guilt, our prayer may become empty words.

Our works of mercy may take us into the midst of war. As editor of The Catholic Worker, I would urge our friends and associates to care for the sick and the wounded, to the growing of food for the hungry, to the continuance of all our works of mercy in our houses and on our farms. We understand, of course, that there is and that there will be great differences of opinion even among our own groups as to how much collaboration we can have with the government in times like these. There are differences more profound and there will be many continuing to work with us from necessity, or from choice, who do not agree with us as to our position on war, conscientious objection, etc. But we beg that there will be mutual charity and forbearance among us all.

This letter, sent to all our Houses of Hospitality and to all our farms, and being printed in the January issue of the paper, is to state our position in this most difficult time.

Because of our refusal to assist in the prosecution of war and our insistence that our collaboration be one for peace, we may find ourselves in difficulties. But we trust in the generosity and understanding of our government and our friends, to permit us to continue, to use our paper to "preach Christ crucified."

May the Blessed Mary, Mother of love, of faith, of knowledge and of hope, pray for us.

from "Reflections on War"

(1933)

Revolutionary war is the grave of revolution. And it will be that as long as the soldiers themselves, or rather the armed citizenry, are not given the means of waging war without a directing apparatus, without police pressure, without courts-martial, without punishment for deserters. Once in modern history was a war carried on in this manner—under the Commune. Everybody knows with what results. It seems that revolution engaged in war has only the choice of either succumbing under the murderous blows of counterrevolution or transforming itself into counter-revolution through the very mechanism of the military struggle.

The perspectives of a revolution seem therefore quite restricted. For can a revolution avoid war? It is, however, on this feeble chance that we must stake everything or abandon all hope. An advanced country will not encounter, in case of revolution, the difficulties which in backward Russia served as a base for the barbarous regime of Stalin. But a war of any scope will give rise to others as formidable.

For mighty reasons a war undertaken by a bourgeois state cannot but transform power into despotism and subjection into assassination. If war sometimes appears as a revolutionary factor, it is only in the sense that it constitutes an incomparable test for the functioning of the state. In contact with war, a badly organized apparatus collapses. But if the war does not end soon, or if it starts up again, or if the decomposition of the state has not gone far enough, the situation results in revolutions, which, according to Marx's formula, perfect the state apparatus instead of shattering it. That is what has always happened up to now.

In our time the difficulty developed by war to a high degree is especially that resulting from the ever growing opposition between the state apparatus and the capitalist system. The Briey affair during the last war provides us with a striking example. The last war brought to several state apparatuses a certain authority over economic matters. (This gave rise to the quite erroneous term of "war socialism.") Later the capitalist system returned to an almost normal manner of functioning, in spite of custom barriers, quotas and national monetary systems. There is no doubt that in the next war things will go a little farther. We know that quantity can transform itself into quality. In this sense, war can constitute a revolutionary factor in our time, but only if one wants to give the term "revolution" the meaning given to it by the Nazis. Like economic depression, a war will arouse hatred against capitalists, and this hatred, exploited for "national unity," will benefit the state apparatus and not the workers. Furthermore, to realize the kinship of war and fascism, one has but to recall those fascist tracts appealing to "the soldierly spirit" and "frontline socialism." In war, as in fascism, the essential "point" is the obliteration of the individual by a state bureaucracy serving a rabid fanaticism. Whatever the demagogues may say, the damage the capitalist system suffers at the hands of either of these phenomena can only still further weaken all human values.

The absurdity of an antifascist struggle which chooses war as its means of action thus appears quite clear. Not only would this mean to fight barbarous oppression by crushing peoples under the weight of even more barbarous massacre. It would actually mean spreading under another form the very regime that we want to suppress. It is childish to suppose that a state apparatus rendered powerful by a victorious war would lighten the oppression exercised over its own people by the enemy state apparatus. It is even more childish to suppose that the victorious state apparatus would permit a proletarian revolution to break out in the defeated country without drowning it immediately in blood. As for bourgeois democracy being annihilated by fascism, a war would not do away with this threat but would reinforce and extend the causes that now render it possible.

It seems that, generally speaking, history is more and more forcing every political actor to choose between aggravating the oppression exercised by the various state apparatuses and carrying on a merciless struggle against these apparatuses in order to shatter them. Indeed, the almost insoluble difficulties presenting themselves nowadays almost justify the pure and simple abandonment of the struggle. But if we are not to renounce all action, we must understand that we can struggle against the state apparatus only inside the country. And notably in case of war, we must choose between hindering the functioning of the military machine of which we are ourselves so many cogs and blindly aiding that machine to continue to crush human lives.

Thus Karl Liebknecht's famous words, "The main enemy is at home," take on their full significance and are revealed to be applicable to all wars in which soldiers are reduced to the condition of passive matter in the hands of a bureaucratic and military apparatus. This means that as long as the present war technique continues, these words apply to any war, absolutely speaking. And in our time we cannot foresee the advent of another technique. In production as in war, the increasingly collective manner with which forces are operated has not modified the essentially individual functions of decision and management. It has only placed more and more of the hands and lives of the mass at the disposal of the commanding apparatuses.

Until we discover how to avoid in the very act of production or of fighting, the domination of an apparatus over the mass, so long every revolutionary attempt will have in it something of the hopeless. For if we do know what system of production and combat we aspire with all our heart to destroy, we do not know what acceptable system could replace it. Furthermore, every attempt at reform appears puerile in face of the blind necessities implied in the operation of the monstrous social machine. Our society resembles an immense machine that ceaselessly snatches and devours human beings and which no one knows how to master. And they who sacrifice themselves for social progress are like persons who try to catch hold of the wheels and the transmission belts in order to stop the machine and are destroyed in their attempts.

But the impotence one feels today—an impotence we should never consider permanent—does not excuse one from remaining true to one's self, nor does it excuse capitulation to the enemy, whatever mask he may wear. Whether the mask is labeled fascism, democracy, or dictatorship of the proletariat, our great adversary remains The Apparatus—the bureaucracy, the police, the military. Not the one facing us across the frontier or the battle lines, which is not so much our enemy as our brothers' enemy, but the one that calls itself our protector and makes us its slaves. No matter what the circumstances, the worst betrayal will always be to subordinate ourselves to this Apparatus, and to trample underfoot, in its service, all human values in ourselves and in others.

Simone Weil

Albert Camus

Neither Victims nor Executioners

(1946)

The Century of Fear

The 17th century was the century of mathematics, the 18th that of the physical sciences, and the 19th that of biology. Our 20th century is the century of fear. I will be told that fear is not a science. But science must be somewhat involved since its latest theoretical advances have brought it to the point of negating itself while its perfected technology threatens the globe itself with destruction. Moreover, although fear itself cannot be considered a science, it is certainly a technique.

The most striking feature of the world we live in is that most of its inhabitants—with the exception of pietists of various kinds—are cut off from the future. Life has no validity unless it can project itself toward the future, can ripen and progress. Living against a wall is a dog's life. True—and the men of my generation, those who are going into the factories and the colleges, have lived and are living more and more like dogs.

This is not the first time, of course, that men have confronted a future materially closed to them. But hitherto they have been able to transcend the dilemma by words, by protests, by appealing to other values which lent them hope. Today no one speaks any more (except those who repeat themselves) because history seems to be in the grip of blind and deaf forces which will heed neither cries of warning, nor advice, nor entreaties. The years we have gone through have killed something in us.

And that something is simply the old confidence man had in himself, which led him to believe that he could always elicit human reactions from another man if he spoke to him in the language of a common humanity. We have seen men lie, degrade, kill, deport, torture—and each time it was not possible to persuade them not to do these things because they were sure of themselves and because one cannot appeal to an abstraction, i.e., the representative of an ideology.

Mankind's long dialogue has just come to an end. And naturally a man with whom one cannot reason is a man to be feared. The result is that—besides those who have not spoken out because they thought it useless—a vast conspiracy of silence has spread all about us, a conspiracy accepted by those who are frightened and who rationalize their fears in order to hide them from themselves, a conspiracy fostered by those whose interest it is to do so. "You shouldn't talk about the Russian culture purge—it helps reaction." "Don't mention the Anglo-American support of Franco—it encourages Communism." Fear is certainly a technique.

What with the general fear of a war now being prepared by all nations and the specific fear of murderous ideologies, who can deny that we live in a state of terror? We live in terror because persuasion is no longer possible; because man has been wholly submerged in History; because he can no longer tap that part of his nature, as real as the historical part, which he recaptures in contemplating the beauty of nature and of human faces; because we live in a world of abstractions, of bureaus and machines, of absolute ideas and of crude messianism. We suffocate among people who think they are absolutely right, whether in their machines or in their ideas. And for all who can live only in an atmosphere of human dialogue and sociability, this silence is the end of the world.

To emerge from this terror, we must be able to reflect and to act accordingly. But an atmosphere of terror hardly encourages reflection. I believe, however, that instead of simply blaming everything on this fear, we should consider it as one of the basic factors in the situation, and try to do something about it. No task is more important. For it involves the fate of a considerable number of Europeans who, fed up with the lies and violence, deceived in their dearest hopes and repelled by the idea of killing their fellow men in order to convince them, likewise repudiate the idea of themselves being convinced that way. And yet such is the alternative

Albert Camus

that at present confronts so many of us in Europe who are not of any party—or ill at ease in the party we have chosen—who doubt socialism has been realized in Russia or liberalism in America, who grant to each side the right to affirm its truth but refuse it the right to impose it by murder, individual or collective. Among the powerful of today, these are the men without a kingdom. Their viewpoint will not be recognized (and I say "recognized," not "triumph"), nor will they recover their kingdom until they come to know precisely what they want and proclaim it directly and boldly enough to make their words a stimulus to action. And if an atmosphere of fear does not encourage accurate thinking, then they must first of all come to terms with fear.

To come to terms, one must understand what fear means: what it implies and what it rejects. It implies and rejects the same fact: a world where murder is legitimate, and where human life is considered trifling. This is the great political question of our times, and before dealing with other issues, one must take a position on it. Before anything can be done, two questions must be put: "Do you or do you not, directly or indirectly, want to be killed or assaulted? Do you or do you not, directly or indirectly, want to kill or assault?" All who say No to both these questions are automatically committed to a series of consequences which must modify their way of posing the problem. My aim here is to clarify two or three of these consequences.

Saving Our Skins

I once said that, after the experiences of the last two years, I could no longer hold to any truth which might oblige me, directly or indirectly, to demand a man's life. Certain friends whom I respected retorted that I was living in Utopia, that there was no political truth which could not one day reduce us to such an extremity, and that we must therefore either run the risk of this extremity or else simply put up with the world as it is.

They argued the point most forcefully. But I think they were able to put such force into it only because they were unable to really *imagine* other people's death. It is a freak of the times. We make love by telephone, we work not on matter but on machines, and we kill and are killed by proxy. We gain in cleanliness, but lose in understanding.

But the argument has another, indirect meaning: it poses the question of Utopia. People like myself want not a world in which murder no longer exists (we are not so crazy as that!) but rather one in which murder is not legitimate. Here indeed we are Utopian—and contradictory. For we do live, it is true, in a world where murder is legitimate, and we ought to change it if we do not like it. But it appears that we cannot change it without risking murder. Murder thus throws us back on murder, and we will continue to live in terror whether we accept the fact with resignation or wish to abolish it by means which merely replace one terror with another.

It seems to me every one should think this over. For what strikes me, in the midst of polemics, threats and outbursts of violence, is the fundamental good will of every one. From Right to Left, every one, with the exception of a few swindlers, believes that his particular truth is the one to make men happy. And yet the combination of all these good intentions has produced the present infernal world, where men are killed, threatened and deported, where war is prepared, where one cannot speak freely without being insulted or betrayed. Thus if people like ourselves live in a state of contradiction, we are not the only ones, and those who accuse us of Utopianism are possibly themselves also living in a Utopia, a different one but perhaps a more costly one in the end.

Let us, then, admit that our refusal to legitimize murder forces us to reconsider our whole idea of Utopia. This much seems clear: Utopia is whatever is in contradiction with reality. From this standpoint, it would be completely Utopian to wish that men should no longer kill each other. That would be absolute Utopia. But a much sounder Utopia is that which insists that murder be no longer legitimized. Indeed, the Marxian and the capitalist ideologies, both based on the idea of progress, both certain that the application of their principles must inevitably bring about a harmonious society, are Utopian to a much greater degree. Furthermore, they are both at the moment costing us dearly.

We may therefore conclude, practically, that in the next few years the struggle will be not between the forces of Utopia and the forces of reality, but between different Utopias which are attempting to be born into reality. It will be simply a matter of choosing the least costly among them. I am convinced that we can no longer reasonably hope to save everything, but that we can at least propose to save our skins, so that *a* future, if not *the* future, remains a possibility.

Thus (1) to refuse to sanction murder is no more Utopian than the "realistic" ideologies of our day, and (2) the whole point is whether these latter are more or less costly. It may, therefore, be useful to try to define, in Utopian terms, the conditions which are needed to bring about the pacification of men and nations. This line of thought, assuming it is carried on without fear and without pretensions, may help to create the preconditions for clear thinking and a provisional agreement between men who want to be neither victims nor executioners. In what follows, the attempt will be not to work out a complete position, but simply to correct some current misconceptions and to pose the question of Utopia as accurately as possible. The attempt, in short, will be to define the conditions for a political position that is modest—i.e., free of messianism and disencumbered of nostalgia for an earthly paradise.

The Self-Deception of the Socialists

If we agree that we have lived for ten years in a state of terror and still so live, and that this terror is our chief source of anxiety, then we must see what we can oppose to this terror. Which brings up the question of socialism. For terror is legitimized only if we assent to the principle: "the end justifies the means." And this principle in turn may be accepted only if the effectiveness of an action is posed as an absolute end, as in nihilistic ideologies (anything goes, success is the only thing worth talking about), or in those philosophies which make History an absolute end (Hegel, followed by Marx: the end being a classless society, everything is good that leads to it).

Such is the problem confronting French Socialists, for example. They are bothered by scruples. Violence and oppression, of which they had hitherto only a theoretical idea, they have now seen at first hand. And they have had to ask themselves whether, as their philosophy requires, they would consent to use that violence themselves, even as a temporary expedient and for a quite different end. The author of a recent preface to Saint-Just, speaking of men of an earlier age who had similar scruples, wrote contemptuously: "They recoiled in the face of horrors."

True enough. And so they deserved to be despised by strong, superior spirits who could live among horrors without flinching. But all the same, they gave a voice to the agonized appeal of commonplace spirits like ourselves, the millions who constitute the raw material of History and must someday be taken into account, despite all contempt.

A more important task, I think, is to try to understand the state of contradiction and confusion in which our Socialists now exist. We have not thought enough about the moral crisis of French Socialism, as expressed, for example, in a recent party congress. It is clear that our Socialists, under the influence of Léon Blum and even more under the pressure of events, have preoccupied themselves much more with moral questions (the end does not justify all means) than in the past. Quite properly, they wanted to base themselves on principles which rise superior to murder. It is also clear that these same Socialists want to preserve Marxian doctrine, some because they think one cannot be revolutionary without being Marxist, others, by fidelity to party tradition, which tells them that one cannot be socialist without being Marxist. The chief task of the last party congress was to reconcile the desire for a morality superior to murder with the determination to remain faithful to Marxism. But one cannot reconcile what is irreconcilable.

For if it is clear that Marxism is true and there is logic in History, then political realism is legitimate. It is equally clear that if the moral values extolled by the Socialist Party are legitimate, then Marxism is absolutely false since it claims to be absolutely true. From this point of view, the famous "going beyond" Marxism in an idealistic and humanitarian direction is a joke and an idle dream. It is impossible to "go beyond" Marx, for he himself carried his thought to its extreme logical consequences. The Communists have a solid logical basis for using the lies and the violence which the Socialists reject, and the basis is that very dialectic which the Socialists want to preserve. It is therefore hardly surprising that the Socialist congress ended by simply putting forward simultaneously two contradictory positions—a conclusion whose sterility appears in the results of the recent elections.

This way, confusion will never end. A choice was necessary, and the Socialists would not or could not choose.

I have chosen this example not to score off the Socialists but to illus-

Albert Camus

trate the paradoxes among which we live. To score off the Socialists, one would have to be superior to them. This is not yet the case. On the contrary, I think this contradiction is common to all those of whom I speak, those who want a society which we can both enjoy and respect; those who want men to be both free and just, but who hesitate between a freedom in which they know justice is finally betrayed and a justice in which they see freedom suppressed from the first. Those who know What Is To Be Done or What Is To Be Thought make fun of this intolerable anguish. But I think it would be better, instead of jeering at it, to try to understand and clarify this anguish, see what it means, interpret its quasi-total rejection of a world which provokes it, and trace out the feeble hope that suffuses it.

A hope that is grounded precisely in this contradiction, since it forces—or will force—the Socialists to make a choice. They will either admit that the end justifies the means, in which case murder can be legitimized; or else, they will reject Marxism as an absolute philosophy, confining themselves to its critical aspect, which is often valuable. If they choose the first, their moral crisis will be ended, and their position will be unambiguous. If the second, they will exemplify the way our period marks the end of ideologies, that is, of absolute Utopias which destroy themselves, in History, by the price they ultimately exact. It will then be necessary to choose a more modest and less costly Utopia. At least it is in these terms that the refusal to legitimize murder forces us to pose the problem.

Yes, that is the question we must put, and no one, I think, will venture to answer it lightly.

Parody of Revolution

Since August 1944, everybody talks about revolution, and quite sincerely too. But sincerity is not in itself a virtue: some kinds are so confused that they are worse than lies. Not the language of the heart but merely that of clear thinking is what we need today. Ideally, a revolution is a change in political and economic institutions in order to introduce more freedom and justice; practically, it is a complex of historical events, often undesirable ones, which brings about the happy transformation.

Can one say that we use this word today in its classical sense? When people nowadays hear the word "revolution," they think of a change in property relations (generally collectivization) which may be brought about either by majority legislation or by a minority coup.

This concept obviously lacks meaning in present historical circumstances. For one thing, the violent seizure of power is a romantic idea which the perfection of armaments has made illusory. Since the repressive apparatus of a modern State commands tanks and airplanes, tanks and airplanes are needed to counter it. 1789 and 1917 are still historic dates, but they are no longer historic examples.

And even assuming this conquest of power were possible, by violence or by law, it would be effective only if France (or Italy or Czechoslovakia) could be put into parentheses and isolated from the rest of the world. For, in the actual historical situation of 1946, a change in our own property system would involve, to give only one example, such consequences to our American credits that our economy would be threatened with ruin. A right-wing coup would be no more successful, because of Russia with her millions of French Communist voters and her position as the dominant continental power. The truth is—excuse me for stating openly what every one knows and no one says—the truth is that we French are not free to make a revolution. Or at least that we can be no longer revolutionary all by ourselves, since there no longer exists any policy, conservative or socialist, which can operate exclusively within a national framework.

Thus we can only speak of world revolution. The revolution will be made on a world scale or it will not be made at all. But what meaning does this expression still retain? There was a time when it was thought that international reform would be brought about by the conjunction or the synchronization of a number of national revolutions—a kind of totting-up of miracles. But today one can conceive only the extension of a revolution that has already succeeded. This is something Stalin has very well understood, and it is the kindest explanation of his policies (the other being to refuse Russia the right to speak in the name of revolution).

This viewpoint boils down to conceiving of Europe and the West as a single nation in which a powerful and well-armed minority is struggling to take power. But if the conservative forces—in this case the USA—are equally well armed, clearly the idea of revolution is replaced by that of

Albert Camus

ideological warfare. More precisely, world revolution today involves a very great danger of war. Every future revolution will be a foreign revolution. It will begin with a military occupation—or, what comes to the same thing, the blackmail threat of one. And it will become significant only when the occupying power has conquered the rest of the world.

Inside national boundaries, revolutions have already been costly enough—a cost that has been accepted because of the progress they are assumed to bring. Today the cost of a world war must be weighed against the progress that may be hoped for from either Russia or America gaining world power. And I think it of first importance that such a balance be struck, and that for once we use a little imagination about what this globe, where already thirty million fresh corpses lie, will be like after a cataclysm which will cost us ten times as many.

Note that this is a truly objective approach, taking account only of reality without bringing in ideological or sentimental considerations. It should give pause to those who talk lightly of revolution. The *present-day* content of this word must be accepted or rejected as a whole. If it be accepted, then one must recognize a conscious responsibility for the coming war. If rejected, then one must either come out for the status quo—which is a mood of absolute Utopia insofar as it assumes the "freezing" of history—or else give a new content to the word "revolution," which means assenting to what might be called relative Utopia. Those who want to change the world must, it seems to me, now choose between the charnel house threatened by the impossible dream of history suddenly struck motionless, and the acceptance of a relative Utopia which gives some leeway to action and to mankind. Relative Utopia is the only realistic choice; it is our last frail hope of saving our skins.

International Democracy and Dictatorship

We know today that there are no more islands, that frontiers are just lines on a map. We know that in a steadily accelerating world, where the Atlantic is crossed in less than a day and Moscow speaks to Washington in a few minutes, we are forced into fraternity—or complicity. The forties have taught us that an injury done a student in Prague strikes down simultaneously a worker in Clichy, that blood shed on the banks of a Central European river brings a Texas farmer to spill his own blood in the Ardennes, which he sees for the first time. There is no suffering, no torture anywhere in the world which does not affect our everyday lives.

Many Americans would like to go on living closed off in their own society, which they find good. Many Russians perhaps would like to carry on their Statist experiment holding aloof from the capitalist world. They cannot do so, nor will they ever again be able to do so. Likewise, no economic problem, however minor it appears, can be solved outside the comity of nations. Europe's bread is in Buenos Aires. Siberian machinetools are made in Detroit. Today, tragedy is collective.

We know, then, without a shadow of a doubt, that the new order we seek cannot be merely national, or even continental; certainly not occidental nor oriental. It must be universal. No longer can we hope for anything from partial solutions or concessions. We are living in a state of compromise, i.e, anguish today and murder tomorrow. And all the while the pace of history and the world is accelerating. The 21 deaf men, the war criminals of tomorrow who today negotiate the peace, carry on their monotonous conversations placidly seated in an express train which bears them toward the abyss at a thousand miles an hour.

What are the methods by which this world unity may be achieved, this international revolution realized in which the resources of men, of raw materials, of commercial markets and cultural riches may be better distributed? I see only two, and these two between them define our ultimate alternative.

The world can be united from above, by a single State more powerful than the others. The USSR or the USA could do it. I have nothing to say to the claim that they could rule and remodel the world in the image of their own society. As a Frenchman, and still more as a Mediterranean, I find the idea repellent. But I do not insist on this sentimental argument. My only objection is, as stated in the last section, that this unification could not be accomplished without war—or at least without serious risk of war. I will even grant what I do not believe: that it would not be an atomic war. The fact remains, nevertheless, that the coming war will leave humanity so mutilated and impoverished that the very idea of law and order will become anachronistic. Marx could justify, as he did, the war of 1870, for it was a provincial war fought with Chassepot rifles. In the Marxian perspective, a hundred thousand corpses are nothing if they are the price of the happiness of hundreds of millions of men. But the sure death of millions of men for the hypothetical happiness of the survivors seems too high a price to pay. The dizzy rate at which weapons have evolved, a historical fact ignored by Marx, forces us to raise anew the whole question of means and ends. And in this instance, the means can leave us little doubt about the end. Whatever the desired end, however lofty and necessary, whether happiness or justice or liberty—the means employed to attain it represent so enormous a risk and are so disproportionate to the slender hopes of success, that, in all sober objectivity, we must refuse to run this risk.

This leaves us only the alternative method of achieving a world order: the mutual agreement of all parties.

This agreement has a name: international democracy. Of course every one talks about the U.N. But what is international democracy? It is a democracy which is international. (The truism will perhaps be excused, since the most self-evident truths are also the ones most frequently distorted.) International—or national—democracy is a form of society in which law has authority over those governed, law being the expression of the common will as expressed in a legislative body. An international legal code is indeed now being prepared. But this code is made and broken by governments, that is by the executive power. We are thus faced with a regime of international dictatorship. The only way of extricating ourselves is to create a world parliament through elections in which all peoples will participate, which will enact legislation which will exercise authority over national governments. Since we do not have such a parliament, all we can do now is to resist international dictatorship; to resist on a world scale; and to resist by means which are not in contradiction with the end we seek.

The World Speeds Up

As every one knows, political thought today lags more and more behind events. Thus the French fought the 1914 war with 1870 methods, and the 1939 war with 1918 methods. Antiquated thinking is not, however, a French specialty. We need only recall that the future of the world is being shaped by liberal-capitalist principles, developed in the 18th century and by "scientific socialist" principles developed in the 19th. Systems of thought which, in the former case, date from the early years of modern industrialism, and, in the latter, from the age of Darwinism and of Renanian optimism, now propose to master the age of the atomic bomb, of sudden mutations, and of nihilism.

It is true that consciousness is always lagging behind reality: History rushes onward while thought reflects. But this inevitable backwardness becomes more pronounced the faster History speeds up. The world has changed more in the past fifty years than it did in the previous two hundred years. Thus we see nations quarreling over frontiers when everyone knows that today frontiers are mere abstractions. Nationalism was, to all appearances, the dominant note at the Conference of the 21.

Today we concentrate our political thinking on the German problem, which is a secondary problem compared to the clash of empires which threatens us. But if tomorrow we resolve the Russo-American conflict, we may see ourselves once more outdistanced. Already the clash of empires is in process of becoming secondary to the clash of civilizations. Everywhere the colonial peoples are asserting themselves. Perhaps in ten years, perhaps in fifty, the dominance of Western civilization itself will be called into question. We might as well recognize this now, and admit these civilizations into the world parliament, so that its code of law may become truly universal, and a universal order be established.

The veto issue in the U.N. today is a false issue because the conflicting majorities and minorities are false. The USSR will always have the right to reject majority rule so long as it is a majority of ministers and not a majority of peoples, all peoples, represented by their delegates. Once such a majority comes into being, then each nation must obey it or else reject its law—that is, openly proclaim its will to dominate....

To reply once more and finally to the accusation of Utopia: for us, the choice is simple, Utopia or the war now being prepared by antiquated modes of thought.... Skeptical though we are (and as I am), realism forces us to this Utopian alternative. When our Utopia has become part of history, as with many others of like kind, men will find themselves unable to conceive reality without it. For History is simply man's desperate effort to give body to his most clairvoyant dreams.

A New Social Contract

All contemporary political thinking which refuses to justify lies and murder is led to the following conclusions: (1) domestic policy is in itself a secondary matter; (2) the only problem is the creation of a world order which will bring about those lasting reforms which are the distinguishing mark of a revolution; (3) within any given nation there exist now only administrative problems, to be solved provisionally after a fashion, until a solution is worked out which will be more effective because more general.

For example, the French Constitution can only be evaluated in terms of the support it gives or fails to give to a world order based on justice and the free exchange of ideas. From this viewpoint, we must criticize the indifference of our Constitution to the simplest human liberties. And we must also recognize that the problem of restoring the food supply is ten times more important than such issues as nationalization or election figures. Nationalization will not work in a single country. And although the food supply cannot be assured either within a single country, it is a more pressing problem and calls for expedients, provisional though they may be.

And so this viewpoint gives us a hitherto lacking criterion by which to judge domestic policy. Thirty editorials in *Aube* may range themselves every month against thirty in *Humanité*, but they will not cause us to forget that both newspapers, together with the parties they represent, have acquiesced in the annexation without a referendum of Briga and Tenda, and that they are thus accomplices in the destruction of international democracy. Regardless of their good or bad intentions, Mr. Bidault and Mr. Thorez are both in favor of international dictatorship. From this aspect, whatever other opinion one may have of them, they represent in our politics not realism but the most disastrous kind of Utopianism.

Yes, we must minimize domestic politics. A crisis which tears the whole world apart must be met on a world scale. A social system for everybody which will somewhat allay each one's misery and fear is today our logical objective. But that calls for action and for sacrifices, that is, for men. And if there are many today who, in their secret hearts, detest violence and killing, there are not many who care to recognize that this forces them to reconsider their actions and thoughts. Those who want to make such an effort, however, will find in such a social system a rational hope and a guide to action.

They will admit that little is to be expected from present-day governments, since these live and act according to a murderous code. Hope remains only in the most difficult task of all: to reconsider everything from the ground up, so as to shape a living society inside a dying society. Men must therefore, as individuals, draw up among themselves, within frontiers and across them, a new social contract which will unite them according to more reasonable principles.

The peace movement I speak of could base itself, inside nations, on work-communities and, internationally, on intellectual communities; the former, organized cooperatively, would help as many individuals as possible to solve their material problems, while the latter would try to define the values by which this international community would live, and would also plead its cause on every occasion.

More precisely, the latter's task would be to speak out clearly against the confusions of the Terror and at the same time to define the values by which a peaceful world may live. The first objectives might be the drawing up of an international code of justice whose Article No. 1 would be the abolition of the death penalty, and an exposition of the basic principles of a sociable culture (*"civilisation du dialogue"*). Such an undertaking would answer the needs of an era which has found no philosophical justification for that thirst for fraternity which today burns in Western man. There is no idea, naturally, of constructing a new ideology, but rather of discovering a style of life.

Let us suppose that certain individuals resolve that they will consistently oppose to power the force of example; to authority, exhortation; to insult, friendly reasoning; to trickery, simple honor. Let us suppose they refuse all the advantages of present-day society and accept only the duties and obligations which bind them to other men. Let us suppose they devote themselves to orienting education, the press and public opinion toward the principles outlined here. Then I say that such men would be acting not as Utopians but as honest realists. They would be preparing the future and at the same time knocking down a few of the walls which imprison us today. If realism be the art of taking into account both the present and the future, of gaining the most while sacrificing the least, then who can fail to see the positively dazzling realism of such behavior?

Whether these men will arise or not I do not know. It is probable that most of them are even now thinking things over, and that is good. But one thing is sure: their efforts will be effective only to the degree they have the courage to give up, for the present, some of their dreams, so as to grasp the more firmly the essential point on which our very lives depend. Once there, it will perhaps turn out to be necessary, before they are done, to raise their voices.

Towards Sociability

Yes, we must raise our voices. Up to this point, I have refrained from appealing to emotion. We are being torn apart by a logic of History which we have elaborated in every detail—a net which threatens to strangle us. It is not emotion which can cut through the web of a logic which has gone to irrational lengths, but only reason which can meet logic on its own ground. But I should not want to leave the impression, in concluding, that any program for the future can get along without our powers of love and indignation. I am well aware that it takes a powerful prime mover to get men into motion and that it is hard to throw one's self into a struggle whose objectives are so modest and where hope has only a rational basis—and hardly even that. But the problem is not how to carry men away; it is essential, on the contrary, that they not be carried away but rather that they be made to understand clearly what they are doing.

To save what can be saved so as to open up some kind of future—that is the prime mover, the passion and the sacrifice that is required. It demands only that we reflect and then decide, clearly, whether humanity's lot must be made still more miserable in order to achieve far-off and shadowy ends, whether we should accept a world bristling with arms where brother kills brother; or whether, on the contrary, we should avoid bloodshed and misery as much as possible so that we give a chance for survival to later generations better equipped than we are.

For my part, I am fairly sure that I have made the choice. And, having chosen, I think that I must speak out, that I must state that I will never again be one of those, whoever they be, who compromise with murder, and that I must take the consequences of such a decision. The thing is done, and that is as far as I can go at present. Before concluding, however, I want to make clear the spirit in which this article is written.

We are asked to love or to hate such and such a country and such and such a people. But some of us feel too strongly our common humanity to make such a choice. Those who really love the Russian people, in gratitude for what they have never ceased to be—that world leaven which Tolstoy and Gorky speak of—do not wish for them success in power-politics, but rather want to spare them, after the ordeals of the past, a new and even more terrible bloodletting. So, too, with the American people, and with the peoples of unhappy Europe. This is the kind of elementary truth we are liable to forget amidst the furious passions of our time.

Yes, it is fear and silence and the spiritual isolation they cause that must be fought today. And it is sociability (*"le dialogue"*) and the universal intercommunication of men that must be defended. Slavery, injustice and lies destroy this intercourse and forbid this sociability; and so we must reject them. But these evils are today the very stuff of History, so that many consider them necessary evils. It is true that we cannot "escape History," since we are in it up to our necks. But one may propose to fight within History to preserve from History that part of man which is not its proper province. That is all I have tried to say here. The "point" of this article may be summed up as follows:

Modern nations are driven by powerful forces along the roads of power and domination. I will not say that these forces should be furthered or that they should be obstructed. They hardly need our help and, for the moment, they laugh at attempts to hinder them. They will, then, continue. But I will ask only this simple question: What if these forces wind up in a dead end, what if that logic of History on which so many now rely turns out to be a will o' the wisp? What if, despite two or three world wars, despite the sacrifice of several generations and a whole system of values, our grandchildren—supposing they survive—find themselves no closer to a world society? It may well be that the survivors of such an experience will be too weak to understand their own sufferings. Since these forces are working themselves out and since it is inevitable that they continue to do so, there is no reason why some of us should not take on the job of keeping alive, through the apocalyptic historical vista that stretches before us, a modest thoughtfulness which, without pretending to solve everything, will constantly be prepared to give some human meaning to everyday life. The essential thing is that people should carefully weigh the price they must pay.

To conclude: All I ask is that, in the midst of a murderous world, we agree to reflect on murder and to make a choice. After that, we can distinguish those who accept the consequences of being murderers themselves or the accomplices of murderers, and those who refuse to do so with all their force and being. Since this terrible dividing line does actually exist, it will be a gain if it be clearly marked. Over the expanse of five continents throughout the coming years an endless struggle is going to be pursued between violence and friendly persuasion, a struggle in which, granted, the former has a thousand times the chances of success than that of the latter. But I have always held that, if he who bases his hopes on human nature is a fool, he who gives up in the face of circumstances is a coward. And henceforth, the only honorable course will be to stake everything on a formidable gamble: that words are more powerful than munitions.

Henry A. Wallace

Are We Only Paying Lip Service to Peace?

(1946)

I have been increasingly disturbed about the trend of international affairs since the end of the war, and I am even more troubled by the apparently growing feeling among the American people that another war is coming and the only way that we can head it off is to arm ourselves to the teeth. Yet all of past history indicates that an armaments race does not lead to peace but to war. The months just ahead may well be the crucial period which will decide whether the civilized world will go down in destruction after the five or ten years needed for several nations to arm themselves with atomic bombs. Therefore I want to give you my views on how the present trend toward conflict might be averted....

How do American actions since V-J Day appear to other nations? I mean by actions the concrete things like $13 billion for the War and Navy Departments, the Bikini tests of the atomic bomb and continued production of bombs, the plan to arm Latin America with our weapons, production of B-29s and planned production of B-36s, and the effort to secure air bases spread over half the globe from which the other half of the globe can be bombed. I cannot but feel that these actions must make it look to the rest of the world as if we were only paying lip service to peace at the conference table.

These facts rather make it appear either (1) that we are preparing ourselves to win the war which we regard as inevitable or (2) that we are try-ing to build up a predominance of force to intimidate the rest of man-kind. How would it look to us if Russia had the atomic bomb and we did not, if Russia had 10,000-mile bombers and air bases within a thousand miles of our coastlines, and we did not?

Some of the military men and self-styled "realists" are saying: "What's wrong with trying to build up a predominance of force? The only way to preserve peace is for this country to be so well armed that no one will dare attack us. We know that America will never start a war."

The flaw in this policy is simply that it will not work. In a world of atomic bombs and other revolutionary new weapons, such as radioac-tive poison gases and biological warfare, a peace maintained by a pre-dominance of force is no longer possible.

Why is this so? The reasons are clear:

FIRST. Atomic warfare is cheap and easy compared with old-fashioned war. Within a very few years several countries can have atomic bombs and other atomic weapons. Compared with the cost of large armies and the manufacture of old-fashioned weapons, atomic bombs cost very little and require only a relatively small part of a nation's production plant and labor force.

SECOND. So far as winning a war is concerned, having more bombs—even many more bombs—than the other fellow is no longer a decisive advantage. If another nation had enough bombs to eliminate all of our principal cities and our heavy industry, it wouldn't help us very much if we had ten times as many bombs as we needed to do the same to them.

THIRD. And most important, the very fact that several nations have atomic bombs will inevitably result in a neurotic, fear-ridden, itching-trigger psychology in all the peoples of the world, and because of our wealth and vulnerability we would be among the most seriously af-fected. Atomic war will not require vast and time-consuming prepara-tions, the mobilization of large armies, the conversion of a large propor-tion of a country's industrial plants to the manufacture of weapons. In a world armed with atomic weapons, some incident will lead to the use of those weapons.

There is a school of military thinking which recognizes these facts, recognizes that when several nations have atomic bombs, a war which will destroy modern civilization will result and that no nation or combination of nations can win such a war. This school of thought therefore advocates a "preventive war," an attack on Russia *now* before Russia has atomic bombs.

This scheme is not only immoral, but stupid. If we should attempt to destroy all the principal Russian cities and her heavy industry, we might well succeed. But the immediate countermeasure which such an attack would call forth is the prompt occupation of all Continental Europe by the Red Army. Would we be prepared to destroy the cities of all Europe in trying to finish what we had started? This idea is so contrary to all the basic instincts and principles of the American people that any such action would be possible only under a dictatorship at home. . . .

Our basic distrust of the Russians, which has been greatly intensified in recent months by the playing up of conflict in the press, stems from differences in political and economic organization. For the first time in our history defeatists among us have raised the fear of another system as a successful rival to democracy and free enterprise in other countries and perhaps even our own. I am convinced that we can meet that challenge as we have in the past by demonstrating that economic abundance can be achieved without sacrificing personal, political and religious liberties. We cannot meet it as Hitler tried to by an anti-Comintern alliance.

It is perhaps too easy to forget that despite the deep-seated differences in our cultures and intensive anti-Russian propaganda of some twenty-five years' standing, the American people reversed their attitudes during the crisis of war. Today, under the pressure of seemingly insoluble international problems and continuing deadlocks, the tide of American public opinion is again turning against Russia. In this reaction lies one of the dangers to which this letter is addressed.

I should list the factors which make for Russian distrust of the United States and of the Western world as follows. The first is Russian history, which we must take into account because it is the setting in which Russians see all actions and policies of the rest of the world. Russian history for over a thousand years has been a succession of attempts, often unsuccessful, to resist invasion and conquest—by the Mongols, the Turks, the Swedes, the Germans and the Poles. The scant thirty years of the existence of the Soviet Government has in Russian eyes been a continuation of their historical struggle for national existence. The first four years of the new regime, from 1917 through 1921, were spent in resisting attempts at destruction by the Japanese, British and French, with some American assistance, and by the several White Russian armies encouraged and financed by the Western powers. Then, in 1941, the Soviet State was almost conquered by the Germans after a period during which the Western European powers had apparently acquiesced in the rearming of Germany in the belief that the Nazis would seek to expand eastward rather than westward. The Russians, therefore, obviously see themselves as fighting for their existence in a hostile world.

Second, it follows that to the Russians all of the defense and security measures of the Western powers seem to have an aggressive intent. Our actions to expand our military security system—such steps as extending the Monroe Doctrine to include the arming of the Western Hemisphere nations, our present monopoly of the atomic bomb, our interest in outlying bases and our general support of the British Empire—appear to them as going far beyond the requirements of defense. I think we might feel the same if the United States were the only capitalistic country in the world, and the principal socialistic countries were creating a level of armed strength far exceeding anything in their previous history. From the Russian point of view, also, the granting of a loan to Britain and the lack of tangible results on their request to borrow for rehabilitation purposes may be regarded as another evidence of strengthening of an anti-Soviet bloc.

Finally, our resistance to her attempts to obtain warm-water ports and her own security system in the form of "friendly" neighboring states seems, from the Russian point of view, to clinch the case. After twenty-five years of isolation and after having achieved the status of a major power, Russia believes that she is entitled to recognition of her new status. Our interest in establishing democracy in Eastern Europe, where democracy by and large has never existed, seems to her an attempt to re-establish the encirclement of unfriendly neighbors which was created after the last war, and which might serve as a springboard of still another effort to destroy her.

If this analysis is correct, and there is ample evidence to support it, the action to improve the situation is clearly indicated. The fundamental objective of such action should be to allay any reasonable Russian grounds for fear, suspicion and distrust. We must recognize that the world has changed and that today there can be no "One World" unless the United States and Russia can find some way of living together. For example, most of us are firmly convinced of the soundness of our position when we suggest the internationalization and defortification of the Danube or of the Dardanelles, but we would be horrified and angered by any Russian counterproposal that would involve also the internationalizing and disarming of Suez or Panama. We must recognize that to the Russians these seem to be identical situations. . . .

We should make an effort to counteract the irrational fear of Russia which is being systematically built up in the American people by certain individuals and publications. The slogan that communism and capitalism, regimentation and democracy, cannot continue to exist in the same world is, from a historical point of view, pure propaganda. Several religious doctrines, all claiming to be the only true gospel and salvation, have existed side by side with a reasonable degree of tolerance for centuries. This country was for the first half of its national life a democratic island in a world dominated by absolutist governments.

We should not act as if we too felt that we were threatened in today's world. We are by far the most powerful nation in the world, the only Allied nation which came out of the war without devastation and much stronger than before the war. Any talk on our part about the need for strengthening our defenses further is bound to appear hypocritical to other nations. . . .

This proposal admittedly calls for a shift in some of our thinking about international matters. It is imperative that we make this shift. We have little time to lose. Our postwar actions have not yet been adjusted to the lessons to be gained from experience of Allied cooperation during the war and the facts of the atomic age.

It is certainly desirable that, as far as possible, we achieve unity on the home front with respect to our international relations; but unity on the basis of building up conflict abroad would prove to be not only unsound but disastrous. I think there is some reason to fear that in our earnest efforts to achieve bipartisan unity in this country we may have

Henry A. Wallace

given way too much to isolationism masquerading as tough realism in international affairs.

The real test lies in the achievement of international unity. It will be fruitless to continue to seek solutions for the many specific problems that face us in the making of the peace and in the establishment of an enduring international order without first achieving an atmosphere of mutual trust and confidence. The task admittedly is not an easy one.

There is no question, as the Secretary of State has indicated, that negotiations with the Russians are difficult because of cultural differences, their traditional isolationism, and their insistence on a visible quid pro quo in all agreements. But the task is not an insuperable one if we take into account that to other nations our foreign policy consists not only of the principles that we advocate but of the actions we take.

Fundamentally, this comes down to the point discussed earlier in this letter, that even our own security, in the sense that we have known it in the past, cannot be preserved by military means in a world armed with atomic weapons. The only type of security which can be maintained by our own military force is the type described by a military man before the Senate Atomic Energy Commission—a security against invasion after all our cities and perhaps 40 million of our city population have been destroyed by atomic weapons. That is the best that "security" on the basis of armaments has to offer us. It is not the kind of security that our people and the people of the other United Nations are striving for.

III. The Cold War and Vietnam

(1950–1975)

A . J . M u s t e

Getting Rid of War

(1959)

Every thoughtful person wants to abolish war and the benumbing threat of nuclear destruction which hangs over all of mankind. The question is how to do it. Here is an attempt to state one answer to that question. It is an answer which hitherto represented the view of a minority; but more and more people are beginning to think it is the only one that makes any sense or holds out real hope.

First, we must try to see the nature of the problem. The international political scene today has two main characteristics. It is marked on the one hand by terrific, dizzying movement in the field of military technology, the development of weapons of extermination. There is, on the other hand, extreme rigidity in the political field, at the point of struggle between the United States and the Soviet Union, the Western and Eastern power blocs.

As for the first, the A-bomb now seems like something out of the Middle Ages in the context of missile development, the firing of satellites to orbit the earth, the catapulting of satellites into outer space—all directly tied in with war preparations on the part of both major powers.

As for political relationships, on the surface, of course, changes occur, or seem to occur, tension waxes and wanes and grows again, and it is clear that at the moment neither power wants a nuclear war; neither wants the situation anywhere to get completely out of hand. But no major political issues, as in Germany or in the Middle East or in the realm of disarmament, get settled. There is no indication that any are on the way to settlement.

I am not impressed in this connection with the struggle that goes on periodically between the White House and Congressional committees over whether a balanced budget or national security is of first importance. These are not struggles between pacifists and militarists, people who want or do not want "genuine negotiation." And however these controversies are resolved, the military budget will still be of astronomical proportions for "peacetime," and intended to enable the United States to obliterate Russia if it should prove "necessary."

Both aspects of the contemporary situation make one think of mass hypnosis, mass hysteria or catalepsy. A short time ago, we were appalled at the thought that some bomber pilot would misread a signal on his radar screen, conclude that an enemy was taking hostile action, and touch off a nuclear war. Now Professor William Pickering, jet missile expert of the California Institute of Technology, points out that it seems inevitable that technological military developments will proceed fatalistically. The calculations now required are so intricate that they have to be made by super-calculating machines. A defect in a tube of such a machine here may lead to a wrong signal being received by a machine in Russia, or vice versa. This will automatically set missiles flying. Even if a human observer realizes in a moment, Professor Pickering warns, that a mistake has occurred, it will be too late to stop the machinery of extermination. Thus, hypnotically, the intricate dance goes on.

In the field of so-called negotiations between the powers, one gets the same impression of mental aberration, flight from reality, in the immobility, the rigid stalemate, the utter failure of diplomats to communicate on controversial issues. Nations simply talk *at* each other like talking machines.

Note that this bound-to-be-catastrophic conjunction of violent movement in one field and stark rigidity in the other goes on, in spite of the fact that the policy makers, generals, scientists, and opinion makers—including the clergy on both sides—know the nature of modern weapons and the character of the war in which they are to be used.

It is essential to note that *in this crucial respect* there is no difference between the leaders in the two rival blocs. Nuclear war is politically irrational and morally an indefensible and hideous atrocity, whoever perpetrates it. Preparation for such war is also politically irrational, and since there is no guarantee that the preparation will lead to anything but war, the preparation itself is an atrocity and a degradation of mankind.

I lay this charge at the doors of Eisenhower and Khrushchev, of Dulles and Gromyko; of the intellectuals of this country and of the Soviet Union and other Communist countries; of the Protestant, Catholic and Jewish teachers of the United States, and of the priests of whatever denomination in Russia.

On each side a claim about the end in view is made by the government, and to a large extent accepted by the people. This claim tends to be absolutistic—that the conflict is an ultimate one, either *the* Revolution which finally will liberate mankind or a war to save "all the values of democratic and Christian civilization." Even insofar as these claims are sincerely made and not sheer propagandist hypocrisy the indictment is not mitigated. Not one of the professed aims of Communism (classless and warless world and the rest) or of the democratic and Christian faith (the sacredness and infinite worth of every human soul, and what-have-you) can be advanced by or salvaged after a nuclear war.

The very arrogance which is revealed in this absolutizing—the infamous notion that *my* regime, *my* country, *my* philosophy is so precious that its defense justifies the obliteration of an enemy people and quite possibly wiping out the population of my own country as well—what can one say of this concept except that it is itself an extreme expression of the mental sickness and the foul moral degradation which has mankind, or at least its present leaders, in its grip?

Note, furthermore, that each of these regimes in the very preparation of nuclear war is alike in displaying the impudence of exposing other peoples and even the future generations of other countries to genetic distortion and death by fall-out and other means. Russia and the United States alike, if war ensues, will doom millions in other nations to death.

This charge, unprecedented in the history of man, lies now at the doors of Eisenhower and Khrushchev, Dulles and Gromyko, and the policy- and opinion-makers of both camps.

In the presence of the stark, central fact of what modern war means, the validity of the talk about defense on both sides—"We do these things because the other side is doing it"—adds up to exactly zero. When mass retaliation is called defense, that is double-think and double-talk on both sides.

Parenthetically, this is not the only point at which both the United States and the Soviet Union need to see that the enemy is not the other nation, but war.

Nor is this the only point at which all of us need to see that the basic fact of international life today is no longer, if it ever was, the battle of the power blocs. It is increasingly the case that each is confronted by the same problems, perhaps in somewhat different form, including the ultimate problems of how the human spirit is to survive and, surviving, to enter into its heritage in the age of the fissioned and fused atom.

Similarly, most of the discussion about which government is making genuine peace offers, negotiating astutely or stupidly, and so on, is also pointless. All this negotiation takes place in the context of the nuclear arms race, and this is an activity of lunatics and global criminals. Neither side gives any indication of being ready to take any risk by withdrawing from this madness. When they stop this senselessness, then we can begin to apply sensible standards to their interminable negotiations.

The situation is so full of peril that many fall back for consolation on the idea of deterrence: the very fact that weapons are so destructive is somehow going to prevent war. Some assert that we actually have a nuclear stalemate now, since general war has not yet broken out.

If the reader will take a historical stance for a moment, he may reflect on what a brand-new idea it is that weapons—the most intricate, expensive and deadly weapons—are made and stockpiled in an atmosphere of extreme tension, for the purpose of never being used. Each big nation turns out this stuff, we are asked to believe, with no notion of ever using it, but simply in order to keep the other fellow from using his. Surely this is an Alice in Wonderland notion. Raymond Gram Swing long ago characterized this as the theory that "the bigger the danger grows, the greater the safety." General Omar Bradley more recently stigmatized it as "peace by the accumulation of peril." Any beginner in logic would point out that if it were guaranteed that nuclear weapons were not going to be used, their deterrent power would vanish.

Obviously, if there were any substance to the concept that we are now secure behind our deterrent shield, we would feel it, a little bit, somewhere. We would relax, take a deep breath. The fact is that the arms race spells tension and creates fear and tension. Brinkmanship is inevitably the foreign policy that is associated with such an arms race, and brinkmanship is not relaxing.

As a matter of fact, neither great power is seeking to achieve a balance. Each is constantly seeking to upset it. In this realm, perpetual motion is the aim. How little intention the "realists," military and civilian, have of breaking out of the fixed pattern of violence against violence was revealed, perhaps inadvertently, by one of the experts of the Rand Corporation (which seems to be a sort of brain trust of the Defense Department), who wrote that if an agreement were reached to "abolish" the weapons necessary in a general war, the need for a deterrent then would be all the greater. For then "the violator could gain an overwhelming advantage from the concealment of even a few weapons. *The need for a deterrent ... is ineradicable.*"

There is, then, no built-in, automatic safety factor in the nuclear power struggle. Modern technology is not equipped with a safety valve. The nature of modern war *may* lead to the abolition of war, provided that men face the facts regarding the abolition of war and the rivalries of power states, and act upon the facts.

All this points to the conclusion that we cannot depend on the accustomed, traditional ways of thinking and of political behavior to save us. We have to find a new pattern of action. There has to be an illumination, a vision. This must lead to a moral and political decision, an act of the will.

It seems to me inescapable, therefore, that we have, as a nation, or a people, to be ready to take unilateral action. Disarmament will not come out of "I will if you will" bargaining; it will come when some nation transposes "war must not be" from the conclusion of an analysis to which everybody agrees into the basis for national action.

We may put this another way: neither the Soviet Union nor the

United States is going to force or cajole or trick the other into breaking out of the circle of suspicion and exposing itself to insecurity in the military power sense. They certainly will not coexist peacefully unless they change substantially. But the change in each case will have to come from within. The one can induce or encourage it in the other only by example, i.e., by unilateral action.

Something like a revolution, a rebirth of man, is necessary and you cannot say to the man across the fence: "I will be reborn, if you will—first." That's something entirely different: a bargain, a deal, not rebirth.

In face of all this, an important development in the struggle to end war is the fact that C. Wright Mills, Columbia University sociologist, and one of the best informed and most sophisticated analysts of political affairs, has recently come out for unilateral nuclear disarmament in a book called *The Causes of World War III*. He says, for example, that "the United States government should at once and unilaterally cease all further production of 'experimental' weapons" and move to destroy or convert to peacetime uses its existing stocks. Mills similarly calls on the government to "abandon all military bases and installations outside the continental domain of the United States."

At another point, he nails down the case for unilateral action, saying: "It is less 'realistic' to spend more money on arms than to *stop at once—and, if must be, unilaterally*—all preparation of World War III. There is no other realism, no other necessity, no other end. If they do not mean these things, necessity and need and realism are merely the desperate slogans of the morally crippled."

As soon as anyone starts to talk about the United States unilaterally getting rid of its nuclear weapons, the familiar questions bob up: "Are you going to let the Russians or the Communists run over you? Would they try to do it? Could they?" There are a number of answers to such questions. Here we must confine ourselves to a few.

The first can be found in a reference in Mills' book to one of those courageous top physicists who are on record as absolutely refusing to help equip their own country, West Germany, with nuclear weapons. Said Max Van Laue (not a pacifist), justifying his refusal against the charge that he was playing into the hands of the Soviets: "Suppose I live in a big apartment house and burglars attack me; I am allowed to defend myself and, if need be, I may even shoot, but under no circumstances may I blow up the house. It is true that to do so would be an effective defense against the burglars, but the resulting evil would be much greater than any I could suffer. But what if the burglars have explosives to destroy the whole house? Then I would leave them with the responsibility for the evil and would not contribute anything to it."

In one sense, no other answer is needed. It is our contention that, whatever the provocation or the danger, there is no justification in heaven or on earth for our arms indiscriminately wiping out any other people, men, women, the aged and the babies. If we have no words harsh enough for those who would do such a thing to us, what are we if we do it to others?

In the second place, the one way in which the sane and democratic elements in the Soviet Union would be encouraged, and the dictatorship undermined, would be by a United States which dared to risk sanity, which acted for peace, which established a true, racially integrated democracy here at home, and which backed the democratic revolutions in the underdeveloped countries so that their people would not find the Communists their only source of aid and leadership. In such a peaceful democracy, multitudes in the satellite countries would see an alternative to which they would be irresistibly drawn. By such a peaceful and genuine revolution, the faith the uncommitted countries had in us would be restored, and totalitarianism might be transformed—as it certainly will not be by war or threat of war.

Here I want to call attention to a remarkable declaration made by a world-famous political analyst, former United States Ambassador to the Soviet Union, and head of the Policy Planning Committee of the State Department, George F. Kennan. In his *Russia, the Atom and the West*—probably the most widely discussed book on East-West relations to have appeared in 1958—Kennan writes:

What sort of life is it to which these devotees of the weapons race would see us condemned? The technological realities of this competition are constantly changing from month to month and from year to year. Are we to flee like haunted creatures from one defensive device to another, each more costly and humiliating than the one before, cowering under-

ground one day, breaking up our cities the next, attempting to surround ourselves with elaborate electronic shields on the third, concerned only to prolong the length of our lives while sacrificing all the values for which it might be worthwhile to live at all? If I thought this was the best the future held for us, I should be tempted to join those who say, "Let us divest ourselves of this weapon altogether; let us stake our safety on God's grace and our own good consciences and on that measure of common sense and humanity which even our adversaries possess; but then let us at least walk like men, with our heads up, so long as we are permitted to walk at all." We must not forget that this is actually the situation in which many of the peoples of this world are obliged to live today; and while I would not wish to say that they are now more secure than we are, for the fact that they do not hold these weapons, I would submit that they are more secure than we would be if we were to resign ourselves entirely to the negative dynamics of the weapons race, as many would have us do.

If things get bad enough, as the weapons race runs its predestined course, Kennan would advise us to have the good sense and moral courage to take unilateral action, to follow the pacifist, nonviolent way. We would be safer doing that, this statesman contends, than if we "resign ourselves to the negative dynamics of the weapons race."

But surely the fact is that we are caught now in these negative and perilous dynamics. We are less likely to be able to break out if we get in any deeper. As more nations get atomic weapons, the harder it becomes to break out, the greater is the risk of an irretrievable misstep and disaster. This is the best the future holds for us unless we break away now, before it is too late. Now is the time for the American people to stake their safety on God's grace and their own good consciences and on that measure of common sense and humanity which even our enemies possess.

What is Mr. Kennan waiting for? What are any of us waiting for?

One final word. Whether or not the nation adopts any such course, the question of the personal responsibility of each of us must be faced by us and by our fellow citizens.

In unequivocal terms, C. Wright Mills, in his recent book, calls upon all men and women, but especially the intellectuals and the scientists, to

A . J .   M u s t e

become conscientious objectors. As for the scientists, "they ought unilaterally to withdraw from, and so abolish, the Science Machine as it now exists."

To the objection often heard that "if I don't do a certain war job, somebody else will," Mills retorts that "this is less an argument than the mannerism of the irresponsible. It is based ... upon the acceptance of your own impotence." He concludes:

My answers to this mannerism are: if you do not do it, you at least are not responsible for its being done. If you refuse to do so out loud, others may quietly refrain from doing it, and those who still do it may then do it only with hesitation and guilt ... To refuse to do it is an act affirming yourself as a moral center of responsible decisions ... it is the act of a man who rejects "fate," for it reveals the resolution of one human being to take at least his own fate into his own hands.

This challenge to each human being to take at least his own fate in his own hands in this matter of war is what the War Resisters League and other such organizations have been proclaiming these many decades. I submit that there never has been a time when the challenge came more insistently to each man and each woman; or when it was more appropriate to support the organizations which, in an age of anxiety, apathy and conformity, call on men each "to take at least his own fate into his own hands."

Erich Fromm

The Case for Unilateral Disarmament

(1960)

One cannot discuss the question of what might happen as a result of unilateral disarmament—or, for that matter, of any mutual disarmament—without examining some psychological arguments. The most popular one is that "the Russians cannot be trusted." If "trust" is meant in a moral sense, it is unfortunately true that political leaders can rarely be trusted. The reason lies in the split between private and public morals: the state, having become an idol, justifies any immorality if committed in its interest, while the very same political leaders would not commit the same acts if they were acting in behalf of their own private interest. However, there is another meaning to "trust in people," a meaning which is much more relevant to the problem of politics: the trust that they are sane and rational beings, and that they will act accordingly. If I deal with an opponent in whose sanity I trust, I can appreciate his motivations and to some extent predict them, because there are certain rules and aims, like that of survival or that of commensurateness between aims and means, which are common to all sane people. Hitler could not be trusted because he was lacking in sanity, and this very lack destroyed both him and his regime. It seems quite clear that the Russian leaders of today are sane and rational people; therefore, it is important not only to know what they are capable of, but also to predict what they might be motivated to do.

This question of the leaders' and the people's sanity leads to another consideration which affects us as much as it does the Russians. In the current discussion on armament control, many arguments are based on the question of what is *possible* rather than on what is *probable*. The difference between these two modes of thinking is precisely the difference between *paranoid* and *sane* thinking. The paranoiac's unshakable conviction in the validity of his delusion rests upon the fact that it is logically possible, and, so, unassailable. It is logically possible that his wife, his children and colleagues hate him and are conspiring to kill him. The patient cannot be convinced that his delusion is *impossible:* he can only be told that it is exceedingly *unlikely.* While the latter position requires an examination and evaluation of the facts and also a certain amount of faith in life, the paranoid position can satisfy itself with the possibility alone. I submit that our political thinking suffers from such paranoid trends. We should be concerned, not with the possibilities, but rather with the probabilities. This is the only sane and realistic way of conducting the affairs of national as well as individual life.

Again on the psychological plane, there are certain misunderstandings of the radical disarmament position which occur in many of the discussions. First of all, the position of unilateral disarmament has been understood as one of submission and resignation. On the contrary, the pacifist as well as the humanist pragmatists believe that unilateral disarmament is possible only as an expression of a deep spiritual and moral change within ourselves: it is an act of courage and resistance—not one of cowardice or surrender. Forms of resistance differ in accordance with the respective viewpoints. On the other hand, Gandhists and men like King-Hall advocate nonviolent resistance, which undoubtedly requires the maximum of courage and faith; they refer to the examples of Indian resistance against Britain or Norwegian resistance against the Nazis. This point of view is succinctly expressed in *Speak Truth to Power:*

> *Thus, we dissociate ourselves from the basically selfish attitude that has been miscalled pacifism, but that might be more accurately described as a kind of irresponsible antimilitarism. We dissociate ourselves also from utopianism. Though the choice of nonviolence involves a radical change in men, it does not require perfection.... We have*

tried to make it clear that readiness to accept suffering—rather than in-flict it on others—is the essence of the nonviolent life, and that we must be prepared if called upon to pay the ultimate price. Obviously, if men are willing to spend billions of treasure and countless lives in war, they cannot dismiss the case for nonviolence by saying that in a nonviolent struggle people might get killed! It is equally clear that where commit-ment and the readiness to sacrifice are lacking, nonviolent resistance cannot be effective. On the contrary, it demands greater discipline, more arduous training, and more courage than its violent counterpart.

Some think of armed resistance, of men and women defending their lives and their freedom with rifles, pistols, or knives. It is not unrealistic to think that both forms of resistance, nonviolent or violent, might deter an aggressor from attacking. At least, it is more realistic than to think that the use of thermonuclear weapons could lead to a "victory for de-mocracy."

The proponents of "security by armament" sometimes accuse us of having an unrealistic, flatly optimistic picture of the nature of man. They remind us that this "perverse human being has a dark, illogical, irratio-nal side." They even go so far as to say that "the paradox of nuclear deter-rence is a variant of the fundamental Christian paradox. In order to *live*, we must express our willingness to kill and to die." Apart from this crude falsification of Christian teaching, we are by no means oblivious of the potential evil within man, and of the tragic aspect of life. Indeed, there are situations in which man must be willing to die in order to live. In the sacrifices necessary for violent or nonviolent resistance, I can see an ex-pression of the acceptance of tragedy and sacrifice. But there is no tragedy or sacrifice in irresponsibility and carelessness: there is no meaning or dignity in the idea of the destruction of mankind and of civilization. Man has in himself a potential for evil; his whole existence is beset by dichoto-mies rooted in the very conditions of his existence. But these truly tragic aspects must not be confused with the results of stupidity and lack of imagination, with the willingness to stake the future of mankind on a gamble.

Finally, to take up one last criticism, directed against the position of unilateral disarmament: that it is "soft" on Communism. Our position is

Erich Fromm

precisely based on the negation of the Soviet principle of the omnipotence of the state. Just because the spokesmen for unilateral disarmament are drastically opposed to the supremacy of the state, they do not want to grant the state the ever-increasing power which is unavoidable in the arms race, and they deny the right of the state to make decisions which can lead to the destruction of a great part of humanity and can doom future generations. If the basic conflict between the Soviet system and the democratic world is the question of the defense of the individual against the encroachment of an omnipotent state, then, indeed, the position for unilateral disarmament is the one which is most radically opposed to the Soviet principle.

After having discussed the case for unilateral disarmament (in the broad sense), I want to return to the practical proposition of unilateral steps toward disarmament. I do not deny that there are risks involved in this limited form of unilateral action, but considering the fact that the present method of negotiations has produced no results and that the chances that they will in the future are rather slim, considering furthermore the grave risk involved in the continuation of the arms race, I believe that it is practically and morally justified to take this risk. At present we are caught in a position with little chance for survival, unless we want to take refuge in hopes. *If* we have enough shelters, *if* the "United States' active offenses and active defenses can gain control of the military situation after only a few exchanges," we might have only five, or twenty-five, or seventy-five million killed. However, if these conditions do not materialize, "an enemy could, by repeated strikes, reach almost any level of death and destruction he wishes." (And, I assume, the same threat exists for the Soviet Union.) In such a situation, "when nations are poised at the last moment when an agreement appears possible to end the risk of horrifying war, unleashed by fanatics, lunatics, or men of ambition," it is imperative to shake off the inertia of our accustomed thinking, to seek for new approaches to the problem, and above all, to see new alternatives to the present choices that confront us.

Thomas Merton

The Root of War Is Fear

(1962)

The present war crisis is something we have made entirely for and by
ourselves. There is in reality not the slightest logical reason for war, and
yet the whole world is plunging headlong into frightful destruction, and
doing so *with the purpose of avoiding war and preserving peace!* This is a true
war-madness, an illness of the mind and the spirit that is spreading with
a furious and subtle contagion all over the world. Of all the countries that
are sick, America is perhaps the most grievously afflicted. On all sides we
have people building bomb shelters where, in case of nuclear war, they
will simply bake slowly instead of burning up quickly or being blown
out of existence in a flash. And they are prepared to sit in these shelters
with machine guns with which to prevent their neighbor from entering.
This is a nation that claims to be fighting for religious truth along with
freedom and other values of the spirit. Truly we have entered the "post-
Christian era" with a vengeance. Whether we are destroyed or whether
we survive, the future is awful to contemplate.

The Christian

What is the place of the Christian in all this? Is he simply to fold his
hands and resign himself to the worst, accepting it as the inescapable will

of God and preparing himself to enter heaven with a sigh of relief? Should he open up the Apocalypse and run out into the street to give everyone his idea of what is happening? Or worse still, should he take a hard-headed and "practical" attitude about it and join in the madness of the warmakers, calculating how by a "first strike," the glorious Christian West can eliminate atheistic communism for all time and usher in the millennium? . . . I am no prophet and no seer but it seems to me that this last position may very well be the most diabolical of illusions, the great and not even subtle temptation of a Christianity that has grown rich and comfortable, and is satisfied with its riches.

What are we to do? The duty of the Christian in this crisis is to strive with all his power and intelligence, with his faith, hope in Christ, and love for God and man, to do the one task which God has imposed upon us in the world today. That task is to work for the total abolition of war. *There can be no question that unless war is abolished the world will remain constantly in a state of madness and desperation in which, because of the immense destructive power of modern weapons, the danger of catastrophe will be imminent and probably at every moment everywhere.* Unless we set ourselves immediately to this task, both as individuals and in our political and religious groups, we tend by our passivity and fatalism to cooperate with the destructive forces that are leading inexorably to war. It is a problem of terrifying complexity and magnitude, for which the Church herself is not fully able to see clear and decisive solutions. Yet she must lead the way on the road towards nonviolent settlement of difficulties and towards the gradual abolition of war as the way of settling international or civil disputes. Christians must become active in every possible way, mobilizing all their resources for the fight against war. First of all there is much to be studied, much to be learned. Peace is to be preached, nonviolence is to be explained as a practical method, and not left to be mocked as an outlet for crackpots who want to make a show of themselves. Prayer and sacrifice must be used as the most effective spiritual weapons in the war against war, and like all weapons they must be used with deliberate aim: not just with a vague aspiration for peace and security, but against violence and against war. This implies that we are also willing to sacrifice and restrain our own instinct for violence and aggressiveness in our relations with other people. We may never succeed in this campaign but whether we succeed or not the duty is evident. It is the great Christian task of our time. Everything else is secondary, for the survival of the human race itself depends on it. We must at least face this responsibility and do something about it. And the first job of all is to understand the psychological forces at work in ourselves and in society.

At the root of all war is fear, not so much the fear men have of one another as the fear they have of *everything*. It is not merely that they do not trust one another: they do not even trust themselves. If they are not sure when someone else may turn around and kill them, they are still less sure when they may turn around and kill themselves. They cannot trust anything, because they have ceased to believe in God.

It is not only our hatred of others that is dangerous but also and above all our hatred of ourselves: particularly that hatred of ourselves which is too deep and too powerful to be consciously faced. For it is this which makes us see our own evil in others and unable to see it in ourselves.

When we see crime in others, we try to correct it by destroying them or at least putting them out of sight. It is easy to identify the sin with the sinner when he is someone other than our own self. In ourselves, it is the other way around: we see the sin, but we have great difficulty in shouldering responsibility for it. We find it very hard to identify our sin with our own will and our own malice. On the contrary, we naturally tend to interpret our immoral act as an involuntary mistake, or as the malice of a spirit in us that is other than ourselves. Yet at the same time we are fully aware that others do not make this convenient distinction for us. The acts that have been done are, in their eyes, "our" acts and they hold us fully responsible.

What is more, we tend unconsciously to ease ourselves still more of the burden of guilt that is in us, by passing it on to somebody else. When I have done wrong, and have excused myself by attributing the wrong to "another" who is unaccountably "in me" my conscience is not yet satisfied. There is still too much left to be explained. The "other in myself" is too close to home. The temptation is, then, to account for my fault by seeing an equivalent amount of evil in someone else. Hence I minimize my own sins and compensate for doing so by exaggerating the faults of others.

As if this were not enough, we make the situation much worse by artificially intensifying our sense of evil, and by increasing our propensity to feel guilt even for things which are not in themselves wrong. In all these ways we build up such an obsession with evil, both in ourselves and in others, that we waste all our mental energy trying to account for this evil, to punish it, to exorcise it, or to get rid of it in any way we can.

We drive ourselves mad with our preoccupation and in the end there is no outlet left but violence. We have to destroy something or someone. By that time, we have created for ourselves a suitable enemy, a scapegoat in whom we have invested all the evil in the world. He is the cause of every wrong. He is the fomenter of all conflict. If he can only be destroyed, conflict will cease, evil will be done with, there will be no more war.

This kind of fictional thinking is especially dangerous when it is supported by a whole elaborate pseudo-scientific structure of myths, like those which Marxists have adopted as their ersatz for religion. But it is certainly no less dangerous when it operates in the vague, fluid, confused and unprincipled opportunism which substitutes in the West for religion, for philosophy and even for mature thought.

When the whole world is in moral confusion: when no one knows any longer what to think, and when, in fact, everybody is running away from the responsibility of thinking, when man makes rational thought about moral issues absurd by exiling himself entirely from realities into the realm of fictions, and when he expends all his efforts in constructing more fictions with which to account for his ethical failures, then it becomes clear that the world cannot be saved from global war and global destruction by the mere efforts and good intentions of peacemakers. In actual fact, everyone is becoming more and more aware of the widening gulf between efforts to make peace and the growing likelihood of war. It seems that no matter how elaborate and careful the planning, all attempts at international dialogue end in more and more ludicrous failures. In the end, no one has any more faith in those who even attempt the dialogue. On the contrary, the negotiators, with all their pathetic good will, become the objects of contempt and of hatred. It is the "men of good will," the men who have made their poor efforts to do something about peace, who will in the end be the most mercilessly reviled, crushed, and destroyed as victims of the universal self-hate of man which they have unfortunately only increased by the failure of their good intentions.

Perhaps we still have a basically superstitious tendency to associate failure with dishonesty and guilt—failure being interpreted as "punishment." Even if a man starts out with good intentions, if he fails we tend to think he was somehow "at fault." If he was not guilty, he was at least "wrong." And "being wrong" is something we have not yet learned to face with equanimity and understanding. We either condemn it with god-like disdain or forgive it with god-like condescension. We do not manage to accept it with human compassion, humility and identification. Thus we never see the one truth that would help us begin to solve our ethical and political problems: that we are *all* more or less wrong, and that we are *all* at fault, *all* limited and obstructed by our mixed motives, our self-deception, our greed, our self-righteousness and our tendency to aggressivity and hypocrisy.

In our refusal to accept the partially good intentions of others and work with them (of course prudently and with resignation to the inevitable imperfection of the result) we are unconsciously proclaiming our own malice, our own intolerance, our own lack of realism, our own ethical and political quackery.

Perhaps in the end the first real step toward peace would be a realistic acceptance of the fact that our political ideals are perhaps to a great extent illusions and fictions to which we cling out of motives that are not always perfectly honest: that because of this we prevent ourselves from seeing any good or any practicability in the political ideas of our enemies—which may of course be in many ways even more illusory and dishonest than our own. We will never get anywhere unless we can accept the fact that politics is an inextricable tangle of good and evil motives in which, perhaps, the evil predominate but where one must continue to hope doggedly in what little good can still be found.

But someone will say: "If we once recognize that we are all equally wrong, all political action will instantly be paralyzed. We can only act when we assume that we are in the right." On the contrary, I believe the basis for valid political action can only be the recognition that the true solution to our problems is *not* accessible to any one isolated party or nation but that all must arrive at it by working together.

I do not mean to encourage the guilt-ridden thinking that is always too glad to be "wrong" in everything. This too is an evasion of responsi-

Thomas Merton

bility, because every form of oversimplification tends to make decisions ultimately meaningless. We must try to accept ourselves whether individually or collectively, not only as perfectly good or perfectly bad, but in our mysterious, unaccountable mixture of good and evil. We have to stand by the modicum of good that is in us without exaggerating it. We have to defend our real rights, because unless we respect our own rights we will certainly not respect the rights of others. But at the same time we have to recognize that we have willfully or otherwise trespassed on the rights of others. We must be able to admit this not only as the result of self-examination, but when it is pointed out unexpectedly, and perhaps not too gently, by somebody else.

These principles which govern personal moral conduct, which make harmony possible in small social units like the family, also apply in the wider area of the state and in the whole community of nations. It is however quite absurd, in our present situation or in any other, to expect these principles to be universally accepted as the result of moral exhortations. There is very little hope that the world will be run according to them all of a sudden, as a result of some hypothetical change of heart on the part of politicians. It is useless and even laughable to base political thought on the faint hope of a purely contingent and subjective moral illumination in the hearts of the world's leaders. But outside of political thought and action, in the religious sphere, it is not only permissible to hope for such a mysterious consummation, but it is necessary to pray for it. We can and must believe not so much that the mysterious light of God can "convert" the ones who are mostly responsible for the world's peace, but at least that they may, in spite of their obstinacy and their prejudices, be guarded against fatal error.

It would be sentimental folly to expect men to trust one another when they obviously cannot be trusted. But at least they can learn to trust God. They can bring themselves to see that the mysterious power of God can, quite independently of human malice and error, protect men unaccountably against themselves, and that He can always turn evil into good, though perhaps not always in a sense that would be understood by the preachers of sunshine and uplift. If they can trust and love God, Who is infinitely wise and Who rules the lives of men, permitting them to use their freedom even to the point of almost incredible abuse, they can love men who are evil. They can learn to love them even in their sin, as God has loved them. If we can love the men we cannot trust (without trusting them foolishly) and if we can to some extent share the burden of their sin by identifying ourselves with them, then perhaps there is some hope of a kind of peace on earth, based not on the wisdom and the manipulations of men but on the inscrutable mercy of God.

For only love—which means humility—can exorcise the fear which is at the root of all war.

What is the use of postmarking our mail with exhortations to "pray for peace" and then spending billions of dollars on atomic submarines, thermonuclear weapons, and ballistic missiles? This, I would think, would certainly be what the New Testament calls "mocking God"—and mocking Him far more effectively than the atheists do. The culminating horror of the joke is that we are piling up these weapons to protect ourselves against atheists who, quite frankly, believe there is no God and are convinced that one has to rely on bombs and missiles since nothing else offers any real security. Is it then because we have so much trust in the power of God that we are intent upon utterly destroying these people before they can destroy us? Even at the risk of destroying ourselves at the same time?

I do not mean to imply that prayer excludes the simultaneous use of ordinary human means to accomplish a naturally good and justifiable end. One can very well pray for a restoration of physical health and at the same time take medicine prescribed by a doctor. In fact a believer should normally do both. And there would seem to be a reasonable and right proportion between the use of these two means to the same end.

But consider the utterly fabulous amount of money, planning, energy, anxiety and care which go into the production of weapons which almost immediately become obsolete and have to be scrapped. Contrast all this with the pitiful little gesture: "pray for peace" piously canceling our four-cent stamps! Think, too, of the disproportion between our piety and the enormous act of murderous destruction which we at the same time countenance without compunction and without shame! It does not even seem to enter our minds that there might be some incongruity in praying to the God of peace, the God Who told us to love one another as He has loved us, who warned us that they who took the sword would perish by

Thomas Merton

it, and at the same time planning to annihilate not thousands but millions of civilians and soldiers, men, women and children with discrimination, even with the almost infallible certainty of inviting the same annihilation for ourselves.

It may make sense for a sick man to pray for health and then take medicine, but I fail to see any sense at all in his praying for health and then drinking poison.

When I pray for peace I pray to pacify not only the Russians and the Chinese but above all my own nation and myself. When I pray for peace I pray to be protected not only from the Reds but also from the folly and blindness of my own country. When I pray for peace, I pray not only that the enemies of my country may cease to want war, but above all that my own country will cease to do the things that make war inevitable. In other words, when I pray for peace I am not just praying that the Russians will give up without a struggle and let us have our own way. I am praying that both we and the Russians may somehow be restored to sanity and learn how to work out our problems, as best we can, together instead of preparing for global suicide.

I am fully aware that this sounds utterly sentimental, archaic and out of tune with an age of science. But I would like to submit that pseudo-scientific thinking in politics and sociology have so far less than this to offer. One thing I would like to add in all fairness is that the atomic scientists themselves are quite often the ones most concerned about the ethics of the situation, and that they are among the few who dare to open their mouths from time to time and say something about it. But who on earth listens?

If men really wanted peace they would sincerely ask God for it and He would give it to them. But why should He give the world a peace which it does not really desire? The peace the world pretends to desire is really no peace at all.

To some men peace merely means the liberty to exploit other people without fear of retaliation or interference. To others peace means the freedom to rob brothers without interruption. To still others it means the leisure to devour the goods of the earth without being compelled to interrupt their pleasures to feed those whom their greed is starving. And to practically everybody peace simply means the absence of any physical violence that might cast a shadow over lives devoted to the satisfaction of their animal appetites for comfort and pleasure.

Many men like these have asked God for what they thought was "peace" and wondered why their prayer was not answered. They could not understand that it actually *was* answered. God left them with what they desired, for their idea of peace was only another form of war. The "cold war" is simply the normal consequence of our corruption of peace based on a policy of "every man for himself" in ethics, economics and political life. It is absurd to hope for a solid peace based on fictions and illusions!

So instead of loving what you think is peace, love other men and love God above all. And instead of hating the people you think are warmongers, hate the appetites and the disorder in your own soul, which are the causes of war. If you love peace, then hate injustice, hate tyranny, hate greed—but hate these things in *yourself,* not in another.

Thomas Merton

Rajendra Prasad

The Way to Disarmament

(1962)

From time immemorial man has been known to quarrel with man, employing such weapons as were available to him at the time. The emphasis has gradually shifted from personal bravery to the efficiency and destructiveness of the weapons. The result has been gradual progress from the ax to the atom bomb. At the same time man has not only lost much of his heroism and chivalry but his conscience has become more and more deadened to the finer feeling of humanity. War is fast becoming a push-button affair. The question therefore naturally arises: how is humanity to be saved from the destruction which is inevitable if the misuse of scientific and technological advance goes unchecked or unregulated? It would seem that the wheel has come full circle and the *reductio ad absurdum* of the logic of violence or brute force is almost complete. If man has sense he must see that he has not only to cry halt to the mad rush toward the final disaster but that he must reverse his direction. This was what Mahatma Gandhi meant when he said that ultimate nonviolence was the only safe defense not only for the individual but also for nations. To him this was not a theoretical proposition but a highly practical plan. He applied it in the struggle for freedom by India, and, however limited the scope and application of the principle, the objective was achieved.

However, we who have met here have no illusions that the spiritual principle for which Mahatma Gandhi stood will today be acceptable to the world at large. Our objective is a limited one—namely, the cessation of nuclear tests, banning of nuclear weapons and total disarmament. This would, of course, include the banning of the manufacture and use of nuclear weapons and the destruction of the existing nuclear stockpiles.

If it were only a question affecting two combatants, who could fight it out between themselves and destroy each other, one could sit back complacently and say: "If they are so minded let them do their worst to each other and be damned." But unfortunately the very future of humanity is at stake. Slaughter of the innocent and the guilty alike on a mass scale is bad enough. It becomes infinitely worse if not only the living but also many generations of those yet to be born are doomed to be afflicted with congenital physical and mental defects. The nonaligned and neutral people are as much involved as those who are knowingly or unknowingly engaged in the criminal conspiracy of creating weapons and conditions that would spell their own annihilation no less than that of others.

There is no known defense against a nuclear attack once it is launched. The only thing that the target country can do is to perfect a system of instant retaliation that would be able to function even when the rest of the country has been reduced to an atomic wreckage. It can, however, be poor consolation to the victim of a nuclear attack to know that after he has been wiped out of existence a similar fate would overtake the adversary.

It has been said that the only way to prevent a nuclear war is to develop an adequate nuclear deterrent. But the strategy of deterrence can be rendered ineffective by several causes. It may be rendered ineffective by the failure or malfunctioning of a radar warning system, by a misinterpretation of the signal given by it or even by a meteor striking the earth. Any of these things could create the illusion that a thermonuclear war was on and touch off an unintended thermonuclear war. On several recent occasions such a disaster was only narrowly averted. It is said that the moon, at least once, and the flights of geese, repeatedly, were mistaken for Russian missiles. Again, an unintended nuclear war may be precipitated by a sudden nervous breakdown of an important military officer or official. Nor must it be forgotten that a non-nuclear war can easily develop into a nuclear war. Finally, it does not require much imagination to see that if the race for nuclear supremacy continues, nuclear weapons will be more and more widely distributed. When many nations possess such weapons, the chances of a nuclear war breaking out are immensely increased. An irresponsible head of a small chauvinistic state may be tempted to employ nuclear weapons against a neighbor and thereby precipitate a global thermonuclear war.

Even if deterrence succeeds, the mounting scale of expenditure on armaments resulting from the nuclear-arms race will be such as to impoverish the nations concerned and deprive mankind of much of the fruits of scientific advance. . . .

A race for nuclear weapons, if it remains unchecked, can have only three possible results:

It may lead to a thermonuclear war between East and West which will result in the annihilation of whole populations on either side, destroy civilization and turn the world into a radioactive wasteland.

Or, as Bertrand Russell points out, assaults on heavenly bodies by the competing powers may take the place of exploding nuclear weapons in the attempt by each to demonstrate its superior counterforce capacity to the other side. "It may well happen," says Russell, "that means will be found to cause them [celestial bodies] to disintegrate. The moon may split and crumble and melt. Poisonous fragments may fall on Moscow and Washington or more innocent regions. Hate and destructiveness having become cosmic will spread madness beyond its present terrestrial confines."

The insane race for supremacy in thermonuclear weapons may lead to the financial bankruptcy of the countries concerned and turn the whole world into a vast slum inhabited by fear-ridden neurotics.

How is it, one may ask, that with all these disastrous consequences staring them in the face, the powers still engage in the nuclear-arms race? Why cannot they agree to stop the ruinous competition and dump their armaments into the sea? The reason is that both sides are in the grip of mutual fear, suspicion and distrust, and these do not make for sanity. The only cure for fear, Mahatma Gandhi taught us, is faith, for suspicion sincerity, and for distrust, trust.

We have seen disarmament conferences dragging on their weary course endlessly, only to bog down in a morass of equivocation and double talk. Diplomats hold forth on disarmament but are not prepared to abjure war. In the absence of fundamental sincerity, talks at these conferences become a maneuvering for a position of advantage by each participant at the expense of his adversary. It is obviously to the advantage of a power that has attained superiority in nuclear weapons to try to freeze nuclear armaments at their present level. But a rival power that is trying to overtake and outstrip it in the race for armaments would naturally object to this. Similarly, a power that has a lead in regard to the conventional weapons and forces might agree to the abolition of nuclear weapons, but a power that is inferior in conventional armaments will wish to make up its deficiency by arming itself with nuclear weapons. In the same way, a power that has already conducted a sufficient number of nuclear tests and holds the balance of advantage in the research on nuclear weapons can very well offer with a show of virtue to call for a moratorium on further tests to put its rival in the wrong box if it tries to overtake it in the nuclear race, and use it as an excuse for a further series of tests when it is ready for them. A proposition for simultaneous disarmament evokes the fear in the free world that if free nations disarmed, Communism would, by engineering revolutions with the help of its fifth columns in the non-Communist countries, destroy the free way of life and force the Soviet system upon them.

The straightest and simplest way to break through this vicious circle would be for all powers to abjure the use of force altogether, and this abjuration would have to be reflected in their domestic policies. There may be an agreement to enforce collective sanctions, economic and other, not involving the use of force, against any power that violates the agreed code.

If any one country, taking courage in both hands, unilaterally disarmed, it would break this vicious circle of mutual fear and distrust and pave the way for universal disarmament. Such a nation would go down in history as the benefactor of mankind and the world would not allow it to fall a victim to aggression. We have of late seen one African country after another achieve independence, not by the use of military force but under pressure of world opinion. Since India has had the unique privilege of engaging in a successful nonviolent struggle for independence, under the leadership of Mahatma Gandhi, it will be urged that she should set the example, if her appeal for unilateral disarmament is to carry any

Rajendra Prasad

weight. I consider this to be a perfectly legitimate challenge. My appeal is addressed to India no less than to the other countries of the world.

It may, however, be that some other country is better qualified than India to take the lead in this respect and will succeed more quickly than we. Mahatma Gandhi was once asked if he, after fifty years of striving, had not been able on his own admission to demonstrate the full power of nonviolence of his conception, what chance was there for others to succeed even in a thousand years? He replied:

It may take some a thousand years, and it may take others only one year. Do not think that, if in spite of my fifty years' practice of it I am still imperfect, it must take you many more years. No, there is no rule of three here. You may succeed quicker than I.

He even envisioned some Western nation, by dint of its training in discipline and organization, and its martial valor, attaining the goal of nonviolence before India, though he never ceased to hope that India would not allow itself to be beaten in the race.

It is, however, arguable that this consummation cannot be achieved at a stroke. It will take time. True, one cannot jump off a running train. Even a man going at more than ordinary speed cannot all of a sudden stop at the last step. The pace can always be adjusted to the circumstances, provided the will is there and a clear recognition of what needs to be done.

So far as the Gandhi Peace Foundation is concerned, the line of unadulterated nonviolence, or *ahimsa*, is the only line that it can take. It cannot seek palliatives by compromising on this point or by speaking in an uncertain voice for the sake of expediency. World peace is its goal but the means for its attainment also have to be peaceful, i.e., truthful and nonviolent. It cannot associate itself with the use of armed force, even for the attainment of peace....

We must have faith that the free way of life cannot be destroyed so long as it is enshrined in the hearts of individuals who are prepared to die for it without anger or ill will in their hearts. A plan for nonviolent defense, however, can have for its object only the preservation of a way of life that is based on honest industry, and the right to enjoy in full the fruit of such industry, coupled with equality and individual freedom, not a way of life based on exploitation, inequality, class distinction, class pride and class rule.

Far from insuring the triumph of one way of life, nuclear weapons only promise the extinction of all life. On the other hand, instances can be multiplied to show that military defeat, occupation and annexation of a country did not result in the disappearance of the nation or its way of life—Poland, Ireland, Czechoslovakia are there, to mention only a few. During the last World War, resistance movements sprang up in several countries under German occupation. The victims of Nazi aggression realized that capitulation by the forces of their respective governments did not necessarily mean the end of popular resistance to occupation. It was further noted that these movements were most successful where they were carried on, largely if not wholly, by moral, i.e., nonviolent means. An outstanding instance of this is provided by the resistance movement in Norway. Violent resistance, where it was tried, proved efficacious only to the extent to which it was the reflection of moral resistance, or the measure of the will to resist in terms of readiness to suffer, and of the intensity of sympathy and active or passive support for the thousands of nonterrorists.

The employment of nuclear weapons is only a part of the technique of terror. The idea behind it is that if the tyrant can demonstrate his undoubted capacity to exterminate the adversary, the latter is bound to submit. But if the adversary learns the art of dying without submission or a sense of defeat, if he develops the awareness that there is in us something which the armaments cannot destroy and which survives even the destruction of our physical body, the power of armaments, nuclear or other, will be sterilized. For it is not the physical destruction of the adversary that the tyrant desires as a rule, but only to bend him to his will.

At the back of the policy of terrorism is the asssumption that terrorism if applied in a sufficient measure will produce the desired result, namely, bend the adversary to the tyrant's will. But supposing a people make up their mind that they will never do the tyrant's will, nor retaliate with the tyrant's own methods, the tyrant will not find it worth his while to go on with his terrorism. If sufficient food is given to the tyrant a time will come when he will have had more than surfeit.

Rajendra Prasad

This was what happened in our own case. The British could have tried to put us down in 1930 by methods which they adopted in 1857 to suppress the Indian Revolt. But we did not give them the chance, because we were, by and large, nonviolent; and even though our nonviolence was not of the purest type, it worked. Lord Irwin had to declare that his government could not impose "the peace of the grave" on India, even though they had the capacity.

Asked whether the atom bomb had not rendered obsolete the weapon of nonviolence, Mahatma Gandhi answered that on the contrary, nonviolence was the only thing that was now left in the field.

> *It is the only thing that the atom bomb cannot destroy. I did not move a muscle when I first heard that the atom bomb had wiped out Hiroshima. On the contrary, I said to myself, "Unless now the world adopts nonviolence, it will spell certain suicide for mankind."*

A little before his death he was asked by a journalist how he would use nonviolence against the atom bomb. He said:

> *I would meet it by prayerful action.... I would come out in the open and let the pilot see that I had not a trace of evil against him. The pilot would not see my face at such a height, I know. But the longing in our heart that he will not come to harm will reach up to him and his eyes would be opened.*

To provide the antidote to the atom bomb, however, requires nonviolence of the highest type. It may be asked whether this would not make too heavy a demand on human nature. Answering this question, Mahatma Gandhi said:

> *The critics gratuitously assume the impossibility of human nature, as it is constituted, responding to the strain involved in nonviolent preparation. But that is begging the question. I say, "You have never tried the method on any scale. In so far as it has been tried, it has shown promising results."*

... After all, the change in our outlook and way of life demanded by Gandhiji, by adopting nonviolence or *ahimsa,* is not more drastic than that resulting from our going in the opposite direction. It only requires foresight, faith and determination to leave the trodden path and chalk out a new one which would be for the benefit not only of the present generation but also countless generations to come. If we feel ourselves unable to undertake and achieve this at one step, let us at least make a move in the right direction by banning all nuclear tests as a preliminary step toward the removal of the threat to human survival that confronts us today, and thus give humanity breathing time to think out and adopt further steps to rid the world of fear, distrust and suspicion, which lie at the root of violence.

Martin Luther King, Jr.

Declaration of Independence
from the War in Vietnam

(1967)

Over the past two years, as I have moved to break the betrayal of my own silences and to speak from the burnings of my own heart, as I have called for radical departures from the destruction of Vietnam, many persons have questioned me about the wisdom of my path. At the heart of their concerns this query has often loomed large and loud: Why are you speaking about the war, Dr. King? Why are you joining the voices of dissent? Peace and civil rights don't mix, they say. Aren't you hurting the cause of your people, they ask. And when I hear them, though I often understand the source of their concern, I am nevertheless greatly saddened, for such questions mean that the inquirers have not really known me, my commitment or my calling. Indeed, their questions suggest that they do not know the world in which they live.

In the light of such tragic misunderstanding, I deem it of signal importance to try to state clearly why I believe that the path from Dexter Avenue Baptist Church, the church in Montgomery, Alabama, where I began my pastorage, leads clearly to this sanctuary tonight.

I come to this platform to make a passionate plea to my beloved nation. This speech is not addressed to Hanoi or to the National Liberation Front. It is not addressed to China or to Russia.

Nor is it an attempt to overlook the ambiguity of the total situation and the need for a collective solution to the tragedy of Vietnam. Neither is it an attempt to make North Vietnam or the National Liberation Front paragons of virtue, nor to overlook the role they can play in a successful resolution of the problem. While they both may have justifiable reasons to be suspicious of the good faith of the United States, life and history give eloquent testimony to the fact that conflicts are never resolved without trustful give and take on both sides.

Tonight, however, I wish not to speak with Hanoi and the NLF, but rather to my fellow Americans who, with me, bear the greatest responsibility in ending a conflict that has exacted a heavy price on both continents.

Since I am a preacher by trade, I suppose it is not surprising that I have seven major reasons for bringing Vietnam into the field of my moral vision. There is at the outset a very obvious and almost facile connection between the war in Vietnam and the struggle I, and others, have been waging in America. A few years ago there was a shining moment in that struggle. It seemed as if there was a real promise of hope for the poor —both black and white—through the Poverty Program. Then came the build-up in Vietnam, and I watched the program broken and eviscerated as if it were some idle political plaything of a society gone mad on war, and I knew that America would never invest the necessary funds or energies in rehabilitation of its poor so long as Vietnam continued to draw men and skills and money like some demonic, destructive suction tube. So I was increasingly compelled to see the war as an enemy of the poor and to attack it as such.

Perhaps the more tragic recognition of reality took place when it became clear to me that the war was doing far more than devastating the hopes of the poor at home. It was sending their sons and their brothers and their husbands to fight and to die in extraordinarily high proportions relative to the rest of the population. We were taking the young black men who had been crippled by our society and sending them 8000 miles away to guarantee liberties in Southeast Asia which they had not found in Southwest Georgia and East Harlem. So we have been repeatedly faced with the cruel irony of watching Negro and white boys on TV screens as they kill and die together for a nation that has been unable to seat them together in the same schools. So we watch them in brutal solidarity burning the huts of a poor village, but we realize that they would never live on the same block in Detroit. I could not be silent in the face of such cruel manipulation of the poor.

My third reason grows out of my experience in the ghettos of the North over the last three years—especially the last three summers. As I have walked among the desperate, rejected and angry young men, I have told them that Molotov cocktails and rifles would not solve their problems. I have tried to offer them my deepest compassion while maintaining my conviction that social change comes most meaningfully through non-violent action. But, they asked, what about Vietnam? They asked if our own nation wasn't using massive doses of violence to solve its problems, to bring about the changes it wanted. Their questions hit home, and I knew that I could never again raise my voice against the violence of the oppressed in the ghettos without having first spoken clearly to the greatest purveyor of violence in the world today, my own government.

For those who ask the question, "Aren't you a Civil Rights leader?" and thereby mean to exclude me from the movement for peace, I have this further answer. In 1957 when a group of us formed the Southern Christian Leadership Conference, we chose as our motto: "To save the soul of America." We were convinced that we could not limit our vision to certain rights for black people, but instead affirmed the conviction that America would never be free or saved from itself unless the descendants of its slaves were loosed from the shackles they still wear.

Now, it should be incandescently clear that no one who has any concern for the integrity and life of America today can ignore the present war. If America's soul becomes totally poisoned, part of the autopsy must read "Vietnam." It can never be saved so long as it destroys the deepest hopes of men the world over.

As if the weight of such a commitment to the life and health of America were not enough, another burden of responsibility was placed upon me in 1964; and I cannot forget that the Nobel Prize for Peace was also a commission, a commission to work harder than I had ever worked before for the "brotherhood of man." This is a calling that takes me beyond national allegiances, but even if it were not present I would yet have to live with the meaning of my commitment to the ministry of Jesus Christ. To me the relationship of this ministry to the making of peace is so obvious that I sometimes marvel at those who ask me why I am speaking against the war. Could it be that they do not know that the good news was meant for all men, for communist and capitalist, for their children and ours, for black and white, for revolutionary and conservative? Have they forgotten that my ministry is in obedience to the One who loved His enemies so fully that He died for them? What then can I say to the Viet Cong or to Castro or to Mao as a faithful minister of this One? Can I threaten them with death, or must I not share with them my life?

And as I ponder the madness of Vietnam, my mind goes constantly to the people of that peninsula. I speak now not of the soldiers of each side, not of the junta in Saigon, but simply of the people who have been living under the curse of war for almost three continuous decades. I think of them, too, because it is clear to me that there will be no meaningful solution there until some attempt is made to know them and their broken cries.

They must see Americans as strange liberators. The Vietnamese proclaimed their own independence in 1945 after a combined French and Japanese occupation and before the communist revolution in China. Even though they quoted the American Declaration of Independence in their own document of freedom, we refused to recognize them. Instead, we decided to support France in its re-conquest of her former colony.

Our government felt then that the Vietnamese people were not "ready" for independence, and we again fell victim to the deadly Western arrogance that has poisoned the international atmosphere for so long. With that tragic decision, we rejected a revolutionary government seeking self-determination, and a government that had been established not by China (for whom the Vietnamese have no great love) but by clearly indigenous forces that included some communists. For the peasants, this new government meant real land reform, one of the most important needs in their lives. For nine years following 1945 we denied the people of Vietnam the right of independence. For nine years we vigorously supported the French in their abortive effort to re-colonize Vietnam.

Before the end of the war we were meeting 80 per cent of the French war costs. Even before the French were defeated at Dien Bien Phu, they began to despair of their reckless action, but we did not. We encouraged them with our huge financial and military supplies to continue the war even after they had lost the will to do so.

After the French were defeated it looked as if independence and land reform would come again through the Geneva agreements. But instead there came the United States, determined that Ho should not unify the temporarily divided nation, and the peasants watched again as we supported one of the most vicious modern dictators, our chosen man, Premier Diem. The peasants watched and cringed as Diem ruthlessly routed out all opposition, supported their extortionist landlords and refused even to discuss reunification with the North. The peasants watched as all this was presided over by U.S. influence and then by increasing numbers of U.S. troops who came to help quell the insurgency that Diem's methods had aroused. When Diem was overthrown they may have been happy, but the long line of military dictatorships seemed to offer no real change, especially in terms of their need for land and peace.

The only change came from America as we increased our troop commitments in support of governments which were singularly corrupt, inept and without popular support. All the while, the people read our leaflets and received regular promises of peace and democracy, and land reform. Now they languish under our bombs and consider us, not their fellow Vietnamese, the real enemy. They move sadly and apathetically as we herd them off the land of their fathers into concentration camps where minimal social needs are rarely met. They know they must move or be destroyed by our bombs. So they go. They watch as we poison their water, as we kill a million acres of their crops. They must weep as the bulldozers destroy their precious trees. They wander into the hospitals, with at least 20 casualties from American firepower for each Viet Cong-inflicted injury. So far we may have killed a million of them, mostly children.

What do the peasants think as we ally ourselves with the landlords and as we refuse to put any action into our many words concerning land reform? What do they think as we test out our latest weapons on them, just as the Germans tested out new medicine and new tortures in the concentration camps of Europe? Where are the roots of the independent Vietnam we claim to be building?

Now there is little left to build on, save bitterness. Soon the only solid physical foundations remaining will be found at our military bases and in the concrete of the concentration camps we call "fortified hamlets." The peasants may well wonder if we plan to build our new Vietnam on such grounds as these. Could we blame them for such thoughts? We must speak for them and raise the questions they cannot raise. These too are our brothers.

Perhaps the more difficult but no less necessary task is to speak for those who have been designated as our enemies. What of the NLF, that strangely anonymous group we call VC or communists? What must they think of us in America when they realize that we permitted the repression and cruelty of Diem which helped to bring them into being as a resistance group in the South? How can they believe in our integrity when now we speak of "aggression from the North" as if there were nothing more essential to the war? How can they trust us when now we charge them with violence after the murderous reign of Diem, and charge them with violence while we pour new weapons of death into their land?

How do they judge us when our officials know that their membership is less than 25 per cent communist and yet insist on giving them the blanket name? What must they be thinking when they know that we are aware of their control of major sections of Vietnam and yet we appear ready to allow national elections in which this highly organized political parallel government will have no part? They ask how we can speak of free elections when the Saigon press is censored and controlled by the military junta. And they are surely right to wonder what kind of new government we plan to help form without them, the only party in real touch with the peasants. They question our political goals and they deny the reality of a peace settlement from which they will be excluded. Their questions are frighteningly relevant.

Here is the true meaning and value of compassion and non-violence, when it helps us to see the enemy's point of view, to hear his questions, to know of his assessment of ourselves. For from his view we may indeed see the basic weaknesses of our own condition, and if we are mature, we may learn and grow and profit from the wisdom of the brothers who are called the opposition.

So, too, with Hanoi. In the North, where our bombs now pummel the land, and our mines endanger the waterways, we are met by a deep but understandable mistrust. In Hanoi are the men who led the nation to independence against the Japanese and the French, the men who sought membership in the French commonwealth and were betrayed by the weakness of Paris and the willfulness of the colonial armies. It was they who led a second struggle against French domination at tremendous costs, and then were persuaded at Geneva to give up, as a temporary measure, the land they controlled between the 13th and 17th parallels. After 1954 they watched us conspire with Diem to prevent elections which would have surely brought Ho Chi Minh to power over a united Vietnam, and they realized they had been betrayed again.

When we ask why they do not leap to negotiate, these things must be remembered. Also, it must be clear that the leaders of Hanoi considered the presence of American troops in support of the Diem regime to have been the initial military breach of the Geneva Agreements concerning foreign troops, and they remind us that they did not begin to send in any large number of supplies or men until American forces had moved into the tens of thousands.

Hanoi remembers how our leaders refused to tell us the truth about the earlier North Vietnamese overtures for peace, how the President claimed that none existed when they had clearly been made. Ho Chi Minh has watched as America has spoken of peace and built up its forces, and now he has surely heard the increasing international rumors of American plans for an invasion of the North. Perhaps only his sense of humor and irony can save him when he hears the most powerful nation of the world speaking of aggression as it drops thousands of bombs on a poor, weak nation more than 8000 miles from its shores.

At this point, I should make it clear that while I have tried here to give a voice to the voiceless of Vietnam and to understand the arguments of those who are called enemy, I am as deeply concerned about our own troops there as anything else. For it occurs to me that what we are submitting them to in Vietnam is not simply the brutalizing process that goes on in any war where armies face each other and seek to destroy. We are adding cynicism to the process of death, for our troops must know after a short period there that none of the things we claim to be fighting for are really involved. Before long they must know that their government has sent them into a struggle among Vietnamese, and the more sophisticated surely realize that we are on the side of the wealthy and the secure while we create a hell for the poor.

Somehow this madness must cease. I speak as a child of God and brother to the suffering poor of Vietnam and the poor of America who are paying the double price of smashed hopes at home and death and corruption in Vietnam. I speak as a citizen of the world, for the world as it stands aghast at the path we have taken. I speak as an American to the leaders of my own nation. The great initiative in this war is ours. The initiative to stop must be ours.

This is the message of the great Buddhist leaders of Vietnam. Recently, one of them wrote these words: "Each day the war goes on the hatred increases in the hearts of the Vietnamese and in the hearts of those of humanitarian instinct. The Americans are forcing even their friends into becoming their enemies. It is curious that the Americans, who calculate so carefully on the possibilities of military victory do not realize that in the process they are incurring deep psychological and political defeat. The image of America will never again be the image of revolution, freedom and democracy, but the image of violence and militarism."

If we continue, there will be no doubt in my mind and in the mind of the world that we have no honorable intentions in Vietnam. It will become clear that our minimal expectation is to occupy it as an American colony, and men will not refrain from thinking that our maximum hope is to goad China into a war so that we may bomb her nuclear installations.

The world now demands a maturity of America that we may not be able to achieve. It demands that we admit that we have been wrong from the beginning of our adventure in Vietnam, that we have been detrimental to the life of her people.

In order to atone for our sins and errors in Vietnam, we should take the initiative in bringing the war to a halt. I would like to suggest five concrete things that our government should do immediately to begin the long and difficult process of extricating ourselves from this nightmare:

1. End all bombing in North and South Vietnam.
2. Declare a unilateral cease-fire in the hope that such action will create the atmosphere for negotiation.

3. Take immediate steps to prevent other battlegrounds in Southeast Asia by curtailing our military build-up in Thailand and our interference in Laos.

4. Realistically accept the fact that the National Liberation Front has substantial support in South Vietnam and must thereby play a role in any meaningful negotiations and in any future Vietnam government.

5. Set a date on which we will remove all foreign troops from Vietnam in accordance with the 1954 Geneva Agreement.

Part of our ongoing commitment might well express itself in an offer to grant asylum to any Vietnamese who fears for his life under a new regime which included the NLF. Then we must make what reparations we can for the damage we have done. We must provide the medical aid that is badly needed, in this country if necessary.

Meanwhile, we in the churches and synagogues have a continuing task while we urge our government to disengage itself from a disgraceful commitment. We must be prepared to match actions with words by seeking out every creative means of protest possible.

As we counsel young men concerning military service we must clarify for them our nation's role in Vietnam and challenge them with the alternative of conscientious objection. I am pleased to say that this is the path now being chosen by more than 70 students at my own Alma Mater, Morehouse College, and I recommend it to all who find the American course in Vietnam a dishonorable and unjust one. Moreover, I would encourage all ministers of draft age to give up their ministerial exemptions and seek status as conscientious objectors. Every man of humane convictions must decide on the protest that best suits his convictions, but we must all protest.

There is something seductively tempting about stopping there and sending us all off on what in some circles has become a popular crusade against the war in Vietnam. I say we must enter that struggle, but I wish to go on now to say something even more disturbing. The war in Vietnam is but a symptom of a far deeper malady within the American spirit, and if we ignore this sobering reality we will find ourselves organizing clergy, and laymen-concerned committees for the next generation. We will be marching and attending rallies without end unless there is a significant and profound change in American life and policy.

In 1957 a sensitive American official overseas said that it seemed to him that our nation was on the wrong side of a world revolution. During the past ten years we have seen emerge a pattern of suppression which now has justified the presence of U.S. military "advisors" in Venezuela. The need to maintain social stability for our investments accounts for the counterrevolutionary action of American forces in Guatemala. It tells why American helicopters are being used against guerrillas in Colombia and why American napalm and Green Beret forces have already been active against rebels in Peru. With such activity in mind, the words of John F. Kennedy come back to haunt us. Five years ago he said, "Those who make peaceful revolution impossible will make violent revolution inevitable." Increasingly, by choice or by accident, this is the role our nation has taken, by refusing to give up the privileges and the pleasures that come from the immense profits of overseas investment.

I am convinced that if we are to get on the right side of the world revolution, we as a nation must undergo a radical revolution of values. When machines and computers, profit and property rights are considered more important than people, the giant triplets of racism, materialism, and militarism are incapable of being conquered.

A true revolution of values will soon cause us to question the fairness and justice of many of our past and present policies. True compassion is more than flinging a coin to a beggar; it is not haphazard and superficial. It comes to see that an edifice which produces beggars needs restructuring. A true revolution of values will soon look easily on the glaring contrast of poverty and wealth. With righteous indignation, it will look across the seas and see individual capitalists of the West investing huge sums of money in Asia, Africa and South America, only to take the profits out with no concern for the social betterment of the countries, and say: "This is not just." It will look at our alliance with the landed gentry of Latin America and say: "This is not just." The Western arrogance of feeling that it has everything to teach others and nothing to learn from them is not just. A true revolution of values will lay hands on the world order and say of war: "This way of settling differences is not just." This business of burning human beings with napalm, of filling our nation's homes with orphans and widows, of injecting poisonous drugs of hate into the veins of peoples normally humane, of sending men home from dark and bloody battlefields physically handicapped and psychologically deranged, cannot be reconciled with wisdom, justice, and love. A nation that continues year after year to spend more money on military defense than on programs of social uplift is approaching spiritual death.

America, the richest and most powerful nation in the world, can well lead the way in this revolution of values. There is nothing, except a tragic death wish, to prevent us from re-ordering our priorities, so that the pursuit of peace will take precedence over the pursuit of war. There is nothing to keep us from molding a recalcitrant status quo until we have fashioned it into a brotherhood.

This kind of positive revolution of values is our best defense against communism. War is not the answer. Communism will never be defeated by the use of atomic bombs or nuclear weapons. Let us not join those who shout war and through their misguided passions urge the United States to relinquish its participation in the United Nations. These are the days which demand wise restraint and calm reasonableness. We must not call everyone a communist or an appeaser who advocates the seating of Red China in the United Nations and who recognizes that hate and hysteria are not the final answers to the problem of these turbulent days. We must not engage in a negative anti-communism, but rather in a positive thrust for democracy, realizing that our greatest defense against communism is to take: offensive action in behalf of justice. We must with positive action seek to remove those conditions of poverty, insecurity and injustice which are the fertile soil in which the seed of communism grows and develops.

These are revolutionary times. All over the globe men are revolting against old systems of exploitation and oppression, and out of the wombs of a frail world, new systems of justice and equality are being born. The shirtless and barefoot people of the land are rising up as never before. "The people who sat in darkness have seen a great light." We in the West must support these revolutions. It is a sad fact that, because of comfort, complacency, a morbid fear of communism, and our proneness to adjust to injustice, the Western nations that initiated so much of the revolutionary spirit of the modern world have now become the arch anti-revolutionaries. This has driven many to feel that only Marxism has the revolutionary spirit. Therefore, communism is a judgment against our failure to make democracy real and follow through on the revolutions that we initiated. Our only hope today lies in our ability to recapture the revolutionary spirit and go out into a sometimes hostile world declaring eternal hostility to poverty, racism, and militarism. We must move past indecision to action. We must find new ways to speak for peace in Vietnam and justice throughout the developing world, a world that borders on our doors.

If we do not act we shall surely be dragged down the long, dark and shameful corridors of time reserved for those who possess power without compassion, might without morality, and strength without sight.

Now let us begin. Now let us re-dedicate ourselves to the long and bitter, but beautiful, struggle for a new world. This is the calling of the sons of God, and our brothers wait eagerly for our response. Shall we say the odds are too great? Shall we tell them the struggle is too hard? Will our message be that the forces of American life militate against their arrival as full men, and we send our deepest regrets? Or will there be another message, of longing, of hope, of solidarity with their yearnings, of commitment to their cause, whatever the cost? The choice is ours, and though we might prefer it otherwise we must choose in this crucial moment of human history.

Martin Luther King, Jr.

Howard Zinn

Vietnam: The Moral Equation

(1970)

When those of us who would make an end to the war speak passionately of "the moral issue" in Vietnam, only our friends seem to understand. The government continues to bomb fishing villages, shoot women, disfigure children by fire or explosion, while its policy brings no outcry of opposition from Hubert Humphrey, Oscar Handlin, Max Lerner, or millions of others. And we wonder why.

The answer, I suggest, involves the corruption of means, the confusion of ends, the theory of the lesser evil, and the easy reversibility of moral indignation in a species which is aroused to violence by symbols. To explain all this, however, is to get involved in a discussion of dangerous questions, which many people in the protest movement avoid by talking earnestly and vacantly about "morality" in the abstract, or by burrowing energetically into military realities, legal repartee, negotiating positions, and the tactics of "broad coalition." Yet it is only by discussing root questions of means and ends—questions such as violence, revolution, and alternative social systems—that we can understand what it means to say there is "a moral issue" in Vietnam.

To start with, we ought to recognize the escalation of evil means during this century—a process in which few of us can claim innocence. What Hitler did was to extend the already approved doctrine of indiscriminate mass murder (ten million dead on the battlefields of World War I) to its logical end, and thus stretch further than ever before the limits of the tolerable. By killing one-third of the world's Jews, the Nazis diminished the horror of any atrocity that was separated by two degrees of fiendishness from theirs. (Discussing with one of my students Hochhuth's *The Deputy*, I asked if we were not all "deputies" today, watching the bombing of Vietnamese villages; she replied, no, because this is not as bad as what Hitler did).

The Left still dodges the problem of violent means to achieve just ends. (This is not true of Herbert Marcuse and Barrington Moore, Jr., in the book they have done with Robert Paul Wolff: *A Critique of Pure Tolerance*. But it was so true of the Communists in the United States that the government, in the Smith Act trials, had to distort the facts in order to prove that the Communists would go as far as Thomas Jefferson in the use of revolutionary violence.) To ignore this question, both by avoiding controversy about comparative social systems as ends, and foregoing discussion of violence as a means, is to fail to create a rational basis for moral denunciation of our government's actions in Vietnam.

I would start such a discussion from the supposition that it is logically indefensible to hold to an absolutely nonviolent position, because it is at least theoretically conceivable that a small violence might be required to prevent a larger one. Those who are immediately offended by this statement should consider: World War II; the assassination attempt on Hitler; the American, French, Russian, Chinese, Cuban revolutions; possible armed revolt in South Africa; the case of Rhodesia; blacks in America. Keep in mind that many who support the war in Vietnam may do so on grounds which they believe similar to those used in the above cases.

The terrible thing is that once you stray from absolute nonviolence you open the door for the most shocking abuses. It is like distributing scalpels to an eager group, half of whom are surgeons and half butchers. But that is man's constant problem—how to release the truth without being devoured by it.

How can we tell butchers from surgeons, distinguish between a healing and a destructive act of violence? The first requirement is that our starting point must always be nonviolence, and that the burden of proof,

Howard Zinn

therefore, is on the advocate of violence to show, with a high degree of probability, that he is justified. In modern American civilization, we demand unanimity among twelve citizens before we will condemn a single person to death, but we will destroy thousands of people on the most flimsy of political assumptions (like the domino theory of revolutionary contagion).

What proof should be required? I suggest four tests:

1. Self-defense, against outside attackers or a counterrevolutionary force within, using no more violence than is needed to repel the attack, is justified. This covers the Negro housewife who several years ago in a little Georgia town, at home alone with her children, fired through the door at a gang of white men carrying guns and chains, killing one, after which the rest fled. It would sacrifice the Rhineland to Hitler in 1936, and even Austria (for the Austrians apparently preferred not to fight), but demands supporting the Loyalist government in Spain, and defending Czechoslovakia in 1938. And it applies to Vietnamese fighting against American attackers who hold the strings of a puppet government.

2. Revolution is justified, for the purpose of overthrowing a deeply entrenched oppressive regime, unshakable by other means. Outside aid is permissible (because rebels, as in the American Revolution, are almost always at a disadvantage against the holders of power), but with the requirement that the manpower for the revolution be indigenous, for this in itself is a test of how popular the revolution is. This could cover the French, American, Mexican, Russian, Chinese, Cuban, Algerian cases. It would also cover the Vietcong rebellion. And a South African revolt, should it break out.

3. Even if one of the above conditions is met, there is no moral justification for visiting violence on the innocent. Therefore, violence in self-defense or in revolution must be focused on the evildoers, and limited to that required to achieve the goal, resisting all arguments that extra violence might speed victory. This rules out the strategic bombing of German cities in World War II, the atom bombing of Hiroshima and Nagasaki; it rules out terrorism against civilians even in a just revolution. Violence even against the guilty, when undertaken for sheer revenge, is unwarranted, which rules out capital punishment for any crime. The requirement of focused violence makes nonsensical the equating of the

killing of village chiefs in South Vietnam by the Vietcong and the bombing of hospitals by American fliers; yet the former is also unjustified if it is merely an act of terror or revenge and not specifically required for a change in the social conditions of the village.

4. There is an additional factor which the conditions of modern warfare make urgent. Even if all three of the foregoing principles are met, there is a fourth which must be considered if violence is to be undertaken: the costs of self-defense or social change must not be so high, because of the intensity or the prolongation of violence, or because of the risk of proliferation, that the victory is not worth the cost. For the Soviets to defend Cuba from attack—though self-defense was called for—would not have been worth a general war. For China and Soviet Russia to aid the Vietcong with troops, though the Vietcong cause is just, would be wrong if it seriously risked a general war. Under certain conditions, nations should be captive rather than be destroyed, or revolutionaries should bide their time. Indeed, because of the omnipresence of the great military powers—the United States and the USSR (perhaps this is not so true for the countries battling England, France, Holland, Belgium, Portugal)—revolutionary movements may have to devise tactics short of armed revolt to overturn an oppressive regime.

The basic principle I want to get close to is that violence is most clearly justified when those whose own lives are at stake make the decision on whether the prize is worth dying for. Self-defense and guerrilla warfare, by their nature, embody this decision. Conscript armies and unfocused warfare violate it. And no one has a right to decide that someone else is better off dead than Red, or that someone else should die to defend his way of life, or that an individual (like Norman Morrison immolating himself in Washington) should choose to live rather than die.

It would be foolish to pretend that this summary can be either precise or complete. Those involved in self-defense or in a revolution need no intellectual justification; their emotions reflect some inner rationality. It is those outside the direct struggle, deciding whether to support one side or to stay out, who need to think clearly about principles. Americans, therefore, possessing the greatest power and being the furthest removed from the problems of self-defense or revolution, need thoughtful

H o w a r d   Z i n n

deliberation most. All we can do in social analysis is to offer rough guides to replace nonthinking, to give the beginnings of some kind of moral calculus.

However, it takes no close measurement to conclude that the American bombings in Vietnam, directed as they are to farming areas, villages, hamlets, fit none of the criteria listed, and so are deeply immoral, whatever else is true about the situation in Southeast Asia or the world. The silence of the government's supporters on this—from Hubert Humphrey to the academic signers of advertisements—is particularly shameful, because it requires no surrender of their other arguments to concede that this is unnecessary bestiality.

Bombings aside, none of the American military activity against the Vietcong could be justified unless it were helping a determined people to defend itself against an outside attacker. That is why the Administration, hoping to confirm by verbal repetition what cannot be verified by fact, continually uses the term "aggression" to describe the Vietnamese guerrilla activities. The expert evidence, however, is overwhelming on this question:

1. Philippe Devillers, the French historian, says "the insurrection existed before the Communists decided to take part.... And even among the Communists, the initiative did not originate in Hanoi, but from the grass roots, where the people were literally driven by Diem to take up arms in self-defense."

2. Bernard Fall says "anti-Diem guerrillas were active long before infiltrated North Vietnamese elements joined the fray."

3. The correspondent for *Le Monde*, Jean Lacouture (in *Le Viet Nam entre deux paix*) confirms that local pressure, local conditions led to guerrilla activity.

4. Donald S. Zagoria, a specialist on Asian communism at Columbia University, wrote recently that "it is reasonably clear that we are dealing with an indigenous insurrection in the South, and that this, not Northern assistance, is the main trouble."

One test of "defense against aggression" is the behavior of the official South Vietnamese army—the "defenders" themselves. We find: a high rate of desertions; a need to herd villagers into concentration-camp "strategic hamlets" in order to control them; the use of torture to get information from other South Vietnamese, whom you might expect to be enthusiastic about "defending" their country; and all of this forcing the United States to take over virtually the entire military operation in Vietnam.

The ordinary people of Vietnam show none of the signs of a nation defending itself against "aggression," except in their non-cooperation with the government and the Americans. A hundred thousand Vietnamese farmers were conducting a rebellion with mostly captured weapons (both David Halberstam and Hanson Baldwin affirmed this in *The New York Times*, contradicting quietly what I. F. Stone demolished statistically—the State Department's White Paper on "infiltration"). Then they matched the intrusion of 150,000 American troops with 7,500 North Vietnamese soldiers (in November 1965, American military officials estimated that five regiments of North Vietnamese, with 1,500 in each regiment, were in South Vietnam). Weapons were acquired from Communist countries, but not a single plane to match the horde of American bombers filling the skies over Vietnam. This adds up not to North Vietnamese aggression (if indeed North Vietnamese can be considered outsiders at all) but to American aggression, with a puppet government fronting for American power.

Thus, there is no valid principle on which the United States can defend either its bombing, or its military presence, in Vietnam. It is the factual emptiness of its moral claim which then leads it to seek a one-piece substitute, that comes prefabricated with its own rationale, surrounded by an emotional aura sufficient to ward off inspectors. This transplanted fossil is the Munich analogy, which, speaking with all the passion of Churchill in the Battle of Britain, declares: to surrender in Vietnam is to do what Chamberlain did at Munich; that is why the villagers must die.

The great value of the Munich analogy to the Strangeloves is that it captures so many American liberals, among many others. It backs the Vietnamese expedition with a coalition broad enough to include Barry Goldwater, Lyndon Johnson, George Meany, and John Roche (thus reversing World War II's coalition, which excluded the far Right and included the radical Left). This bloc justifies the carnage in Vietnam with a huge image of invading armies, making only one small change in the subtitle: replacing the word "Fascist" with the word "Communist." Then, the whole savage arsenal of World War II—the means both justified and unjustifiable—supported by that great fund of indignation built against the Nazis, can be turned to the uses of the American Century.

To leave the Munich analogy intact, to fail to discuss communism and fascism, is to leave untouched the major premise which supports the present policy of near genocide in Vietnam. I propose here at least to initiate such a discussion.

Let's refresh our memories on what happened at Munich. Chamberlain of England and Daladier of France met Hitler and Mussolini (this was September 30, 1938) and agreed to surrender the Sudeten part of Czechoslovakia, inhabited by German-speaking people, hoping thus to prevent a general war in Europe. Chamberlain returned to England, claiming he had brought "peace in our time." Six months later, Hitler had gobbled up the rest of Czechoslovakia; then he began presenting ultimatums to Poland and by September 3, 1939, general war had broken out in Europe.

There is strong evidence that if the Sudetenland had not been surrendered at Munich—with it went Czechoslovakia's powerful fortifications, 70 percent of its iron, steel, and electric power, 86 percent of its chemicals, 66 percent of its coal—and had Hitler then gone to war, he would have been defeated quickly, with the aid of Czechoslovakia's thirty-five well-trained divisions. And if he chose, at the sign of resistance, not to go to war, then at least he would have stopped his expansion.

And so, the analogy continues, to let the Communist-dominated National Liberation Front win in South Vietnam (for the real obstacle in the sparring over negotiations is the role of the NLF in a new government) is to encourage more Communist expansion in Southeast Asia and beyond, and perhaps to lead to a war more disastrous than the present one; to stop communism in South Vietnam is to discourage its expansion elsewhere.

We should note, first, some of the important differences between the Munich situation in 1938 and Vietnam today:

1. In 1938, the main force operating against the Czech status quo was an outside force, Hitler's Germany; the supporting force was the Sudeten group inside led by Konrad Henlein. Since 1958 (and traceable back to 1942), the major force operating against the *status quo* in South Vietnam has been an inside force, formed in 1960 into the NLF; the chief supporter is not an outside nation but another part of the same nation, North Viet-

nam. The largest outside force in Vietnam consists of American troops (who, interestingly, are referred to in West Germany as *Bandenkampfverbande*, Bandit Fighting Units, the name used in World War II by the Waffen-S.S. units to designate the guerrillas whom they specialized in killing). To put it another way, in 1938, the Germans were trying to take over part of another country. Today, the Vietcong are trying to take over part of their own country. In 1938, the outsider was Germany. Today it is the United States.

2. The Czech government, whose interests the West surrendered to Hitler in 1938, was a strong, effective, prosperous, democratic government—the government of Beneš and Masaryk. The South Vietnamese government which we support is a hollow shell of a government, unstable, unpopular, corrupt, a dictatorship of bullies and torturers, disdainful of free elections and representative government (recently they opposed establishing a National Assembly on the ground that it might lead to communism), headed by a long line of tyrants from Bao Dai to Diem to Ky, who no more deserve to be ranked with Beneš and Masaryk than Governor Wallace of Alabama deserves to be compared with Thomas Jefferson. It is a government whose perpetuation is not worth the loss of a single human life.

3. Standing firm in 1938 meant engaging, in order to defeat once and for all, the central threat of that time, Hitler's Germany. Fighting in Vietnam today, even if it brings total victory, does not at all engage what the United States considers the central foes—the Soviet Union and Communist China. Even if international communism *were* a single organism, to annihilate the Vietcong would be merely to remove a toenail from an elephant. To engage what we think is the source of our difficulties (Red China one day, Soviet Russia the next) would require nuclear war, and even Robert Strange McNamara doesn't seem up to that.

4. There is an important difference between the historical context of Munich, 1938, and that of Vietnam, 1966. Munich was the culmination of a long line of surrenders and refusals to act: when Japan invaded China in 1931, when Mussolini invaded Ethiopia in 1935, when Hitler remilitarized the Rhineland in 1936, when Hitler and Mussolini supported the Franco attack on Republican Spain 1936–39, when Japan attacked China

in 1937, when Hitler took Austria in the spring of 1938. The Vietnam crisis, on the other hand, is the culmination of a long series of events in which the West has on occasion held back (as in Czechoslovakia in 1948, or Hungary in 1956), but more often taken firm action, from the Truman Doctrine to the Berlin blockade to the Korean conflict, to the Cuban blockade of 1962. So, withdrawing from Vietnam would not reinforce a pattern in the way that the Munich pact did. It would be another kind of line in that jagged graph which represents recent foreign policy.

5. We have twenty years of cold-war history to test the proposition derived from the Munich analogy—that a firm stand in Vietnam is worth the huge loss of life, because it will persuade the Communists there must be no more uprisings elsewhere. But what effect did our refusal to allow the defeat of South Korea (1950–53), or our aid in suppressing the Huk rebellion in the Philippines (1947–55), or the suppression of guerrillas in Malaya (1948–60), have on the guerrilla warfare in South Vietnam which started around 1958 and became consolidated under the National Liberation Front in 1960? If our use of subversion and arms to overthrow Guatemala in 1954 showed the Communists in Latin America that we meant business, then how did it happen that Castro rebelled and won in 1959? Did our invasion of Cuba in 1961, our blockade in 1962, show other revolutionaries in Latin America that they must desist? Then how explain the Dominican uprising in 1965? And did our dispatch of the Marines to Santo Domingo end the fighting of guerrillas in the mountains of Peru?

One touches the Munich analogy and it falls apart. This suggests something more fundamental: that American policy makers and their supporters simply do not understand either the nature of communism or the nature of the various uprisings that have taken place in the postwar world. They are not able to believe that hunger, homelessness, oppression are sufficient spurs to revolution, without outside instigation, just as Dixie governors could not believe that Negroes marching in the streets were not led by outside agitators.

So, communism and revolution require discussion. They are sensitive questions, which some in the protest movement hesitate to broach for fear of alienating allies. But they are basic to that inversion of morality which enables the United States to surround the dirty war in Vietnam with the righteous glow of war against Hitler.

A key assumption in this inversion is that communism and Nazism are sufficiently identical to be treated alike. However, communism as a set of ideals has attracted good people—not racists, or bullies, or militarists—all over the world. One may argue that in Communist countries citizens had better affirm their allegiance to it, but that doesn't account for the fact that millions, in France, Italy, and Indonesia are Communist party members, that countless others all over the world have been inspired by Marxian ideals. And why should they not? These ideals include peace, brotherhood, racial equality, the classless society, the withering away of the state.

If Communists behave much better out of power than in it, that is a commentary not on their ideals but on weaknesses which they share with non-Communist wielders of power. If, presumably in pursuit of their ideals, they have resorted to brutal tactics, maintained suffocating bureaucracies and rigid dogmas, that makes them about as reprehensible as other nations, other social systems which, while boasting of the Judeo-Christian heritage, have fostered war, exploitation, colonialism, and race hatred. We judge ourselves by our ideals; others by their actions. It is a great convenience.

The ultimate values of the Nazis, let us recall, included racism, elitism, militarism, and war as ends in themselves. Unlike either the Communist nations or the Capitalist democracies, there is here no ground for appeal to higher purposes. The ideological basis for coexistence between Communist and Capitalist nations is the rough consensus of ultimate goals which they share. While war is held off, the citizens on both sides—it is to be hoped and indeed it is beginning to occur—will increasingly insist that their leaders live up to these values.

One of these professed values—which the United States is trying with difficulty to conceal by fragile arguments and feeble analogies—is the self-determination of peoples. Self-determination justifies the overthrow of entrenched oligarchies—whether foreign or domestic—in ways that will not lead to general war. China, Egypt, Indonesia, Algeria, and Cuba are examples. Such revolutions tend to set up dictatorships, but they do so in the name of values which can be used to erode that same dictatorship. They therefore deserve as much general support and specific criticism as did the American revolutionaries, who set up a slaveholding government, but with a commitment to freedom which later led it, *against its wishes*, to abolitionism.

The easy use of the term "totalitarian" to cover both Nazis and Communists, or to equate the South Vietnamese regime with that of Ho Chi Minh, fails to make important distinctions, just as dogmatists of the Left sometimes fail to distinguish between Fascist states and capitalist democracies.

This view is ahistorical on two counts. First, it ignores the fact that, for the swift economic progress needed by new nations today, a Communist-led regime does an effective job (though it is not the only type of new government that can). In doing so, it raises educational and living standards and thus paves the way (as the USSR and Eastern Europe already show) for attacks from within on its own thought-control system. Second, this view forgets that the United States and Western Europe, now haughty in prosperity, with a fair degree of free expression, built their present status on the backs of either slaves or colonial people, and subjected their own laboring populations to several generations of misery before beginning to look like welfare states.

The perspective of history suggests that a united Vietnam under Ho Chi Minh is preferable to the elitist dictatorship of the South, just as Maoist China with all its faults is preferable to the rule of Chiang, and Castro's Cuba to Batista's. We do not have pure choices in the present, although we should never surrender those values which can shape the future. Right now, for Vietnam, a Communist government is probably the best avenue to that whole packet of human values which make up the common morality of mankind today: the preservation of human life, self-determination, economic security, the end of race and class oppression, that freedom of speech which an educated population begins to demand.

This is a conclusion which critics of government policy have hesitated to make. With some, it is because they simply don't believe it, but with others, it is because they don't want to rock the boat of "coalition."

Yet the main obstacle to United States withdrawal is a fear that is real—that South Vietnam will then go Communist. If we fail to discuss this honestly, we leave untouched a major plank in the structure that supports U.S. action.

When the jump is made from real fears to false ones, we get something approaching lunacy in American international behavior. Richard Hofstadter, in *The Paranoid Style in American Politics*, writes of "the central preconception of the paranoid style—the existence of a vast, insidious, preternaturally effective, international conspiratorial network designed to perpetuate acts of the most fiendish character."

Once, the center of the conspiracy was Russia. A political scientist doing strategic research for the government told me recently with complete calm that his institute decided not too long ago that they had been completely wrong about the premise which underlay much of American policy in the postwar period—the premise that Russia hoped to take over Western Europe by force. Yet now, with not a tremor of doubt, the whole kit and caboodle of the invading-hordes theory is transferred to China.

Paranoia starts from a base of facts, but then leaps wildly to an absurd conclusion. It is a fact that China is totalitarian in its limitation of free speech, is fierce in its expression of hatred for the United States, that it crushed opposition in Tibet, and fought for a strip of territory on the Indian border. But let's consider India briefly: it crushed an uprising in Hyderabad, took over the state of Kerala, initiated attacks on the China border, took Goa by force, and is fierce in its insistence on Kashmir. Yet we do not accuse it of wanting to take over the world.

Of course, there is a difference. China is emotionally tied to and sometimes aids obstreperous rebellions all over the world. However, China is not the source of these rebellions. The problem is not that China wants to take over the world, but that various peoples want to take over their parts of the world, and without the courtesies that attend normal business transactions. What if the Negroes in Watts really rose up and tried to take over Los Angeles? Would we blame that on Castro?

Not only does paranoia lead the United States to see international conspiracy where there is a diversity of Communist nations based on indigenous Communist movements. It also confuses communism with a

Howard Zinn

much broader movement of this century—the rising of the hungry and harassed people in Asia, Africa, Latin America (and the American South). Hence we try to crush radicalism in one place (Greece, Iran, Guatemala, the Philippines, etc.) and apparently succeed, only to find a revolution—whether Communist or Socialist or nationalist or of indescribable character—springing up somewhere else. We surround the world with our navy, cover the sky with our planes, fling our money to the winds, and then a revolution takes place in Cuba, ninety miles from home. We see every rebellion everywhere as the result of some devilish plot concocted in Moscow or Peking, when what is really happening is that people everywhere want to eat and to be free, and will use desperate means and any one of a number of social systems to achieve their ends.

The other side makes the same mistake. The Russians face a revolt in Hungary or Poznan, and attribute it to bourgeois influence, or to American scheming. Stalin's paranoia led him to send scores of old Bolsheviks before the firing squad. The Chinese seem to be developing obsessions about the United States; but in their case we are doing our best to match their wildest accusations with reality. It would be paranoid for Peking to claim that the United States is surrounding China with military bases, occupying countries on its border, keeping hundreds of thousands of troops within striking distance, contemplating the bombing of its population—if it were not largely true.

A worldwide revolution is taking place, aiming to achieve the very values that all major countries, East and West, claim to uphold: self-determination, economic security, racial equality, freedom. It takes many forms—Castro's, Mao's, Nasser's, Sukarno's, Senghor's, Kenyatta's. That it does not realize all its aims from the start makes it hardly more imperfect than we were in 1776. The road to freedom is stony, but people are going to march along it. What we need to do is improve the road, not blow it up.

The United States Government has tried hard to cover its moral nakedness in Vietnam. But the signs of its failure grow by the day. Facts have a way of coming to light. Also, we have recently had certain experiences which make us less naive about governments while we become more hopeful about people: the civil rights movement, the student revolt, the rise of dissent inside the Communist countries, the emergence of fresh, brave spirits in Africa, Asia, Latin America, and in our own country.

It is not our job, as citizens, to point out the difficulties of our military position (this, when true, is quite evident), or to work out clever bases for negotiating (the negotiators, when they *must*, will find a way), or to dissemble what we know is true in order to build a coalition (coalitions grow naturally from what is common to a heterogeneous group, and require each element to represent its colors as honestly as possible to make the mosaic accurate and strong). As a sign of the strange "progress" the world has made, from now on all moral transgressions take the form of irony, because they are committed against officially proclaimed values. The job of citizens, in any society, any time, is simply to point this out.

Howard Zinn

IV. Post-Vietnam to the Present

(1975–)

Daniel Berrigan and Thich Nhat Hanh

Communities of Resistance: A Conversation

(1975)

Nhat Hanh: Tell me, how do you see the possibility of developing and maintaining communities of resistance in the United States and elsewhere? We have not talked about that.

Berrigan: But, it seems to me, everything we've talked about leads naturally to that.

I think there's not much else other than these communities on the horizon, and not much else worth giving one's energy to. I'm very fortunate in having in my own family and friends examples of such community, and I'm sure you do too. I guess the question is one of encouraging and enlarging all of this; you know, realizing that the sixties are by no means a finished decade but that they set in motion a pattern of violence, as well as a counterforce of nonviolence which must be maintained. I have the deepest conviction that a sane and reasonable religious sense has the resources to bring these communities into being and to maintain them. There are other bases from which to start—but I know this way. I know this is a good way. I know what it can do.

The more I move around, the more I realize that whatever I do should be judged in its relationship to these communities. I think I'm drawn more and more into the understanding that the future, if we want to talk about the future in a real and concrete way, will include this form of community.

Nhat Hanh: I hope to see communities like that everywhere, as a kind of demonstration that life is possible, a future is possible. Someone has said that cities are places where humans are the only living beings; there are no trees, no animals, no other kinds of living beings, no nature. There is a lack of balance. And then there are many things that regulate us, rob us of our serenity, our peace, our time, ourselves. So, a community that shows abundance of life, that is an example of the wholeness of life, would be an eloquent sign of the possibility of the future. I believe that in such a community, one person could signify hope and life sufficiently to maintain the community.

I don't know what kind of rapport such a community could have with existing monastic communities—whether it could learn from them, whether there could be a mutual sharing. In certain monastic communities such changes are under way, in order to arrive at wholeness. What can the church do in order to encourage and support a community life which is simple and alive?

Berrigan: These are very deep waters. I have had these ideas for a long time and never got anywhere with them except with Merton. And it's interesting that so much of his dream waited on his death. It's only after his death that these communities of resistance are springing up in his name, inspired by his writing and his life. But, I would think that the more we can break down the wall between—*monastic* maybe is an unfortunate word because it's not common coin. Community, in our case Christian community, includes degrees of, rhythms of, withdrawal and involvement, withdrawal and urban dedication and international dedication— all of these things. And the worst thing that can happen to monks is that they get convinced that they're different from ordinary poeple. That's very bad on both sides. The worst thing that can happen to Christian or Buddhist laypeople, I would think, is that they begin to say, "Well, the monks are so different that there's nothing to talk about, nothing to share."

Still the walls are there and the walls are high, at least in the West. I must say I have never been attracted to the monastery since Merton died. I never felt that there was a spirit that would be sympathetic to what I was trying for. You know, this is a great tragedy. My friends who have visited the monastery since he died say it's not a very interesting place. And we've appreciated more and more the deep pain of Merton's struggle to try to stay with that community and still to speak to the world. Well, maybe this is not terribly to the point, but the number of monks who are deeply conscious of the pain of the world is small—at least in the sense that they know they have something to offer to heal that pain. This is, I feel, a great loss to them and to us. I have so often said to young monks, "Try to think that you are not planted somewhere like a tree, but are on pilgrimage, back and forth; one who goes and comes back and offers to our people the resources of discipline and wisdom which are your gifts; gifts which, I think, are bottled into a monastery vintage and are simply not available to us." But it is difficult for this to be heard, very difficult.

Nhat Hanh: In our tradition, monasteries are only a kind of laboratory to spend time in, in order to discover something. They're not an end, they're a means. You get training and practice of the spiritual life so that you can go elsewhere and be with other people. In our special situation where the war has been a terrible reality, the monks have really been with the people. Both monks and laypeople have made efforts to find a form of community that is more fitted to our need. A number of friends and I have tried a new community. It was successful because, I think, it grew out of the tradition, because most who came to the community had undergone some training in monasteries. But our community, well, we made it very different. There was absolutely no rule, no discipline.

And we also accepted non-monks—writers and artists—to be residents for months or years. That worked well, I think, because the people who came there had the same kind of need. We didn't need an abbot or a monastic rule.

Unfortunately, the war finally prevented us from continuing. But that too proved a blessing. Many of the young monks and nuns have cooperated with the peasants to form new communities where they work the land like the other people. They also have days and hours of meditation, studies, and recitation of sutras and prayer. Without that it would be hard for them to continue. We also tried a new order, an order that would be easier for the young people to join and to feel at home in. You know, Nhat Chi Mai, the girl who burned herself—she belonged to that order. In that order, you are supposed to have ninety days a year—three months—of contemplative life. But you can space it the way you want it. And each week one day is left free.

Berrigan: That's nice. For flying kites? [Laughter]

Nhat Hanh: Sure! And for reciting the book of discipline, meditation, and doing things you want like arranging flowers, reading poetry, and things like that.

Berrigan: Would you say a little something more about the rule that you decided on?

Nhat Hanh: You know, in our tradition the monk's rules are 250 and the rule for the nuns, 100 more. That's called nuns' liberation! [Laughter] But for the new order there are only fourteen rules.

Berrigan: Ah! That's not too many.

Nhat Hanh: And the idea is different, because they are more like guiding principles than rules. Each principle should be studied and applied with all one's strength. The first rule is about the worship of ideologies. "One should not be idolatrous or bound to any doctrine, any theory, any ideology, including Buddhist ones. Buddhist systems of thought must be guiding means and not absolute truth." There are principles to help us free ourselves from prejudices and listen to others and see reality and truth of different forms. The rule not to kill, however, does not come first.

Berrigan: That's interesting.

Nhat Hanh: The rule says not to kill—not to kill and not to allow or encourage others to kill. And to do all you can in order to prevent killing and to prevent war. Concerning the problem of suffering, it is said in another principle—do not cut yourself off from suffering people, because that contact nourishes one's compassion. We also had a code of disciplines.

All this was to be reviewed every three years so it would fit the current situation. It is the spiritual life of the community that leads to change. The principle is only a manifestation of the spiritual life, and not something that conditions the spiritual life.

I think if we have peace in Vietnam, it still will be possible for us to build communities where we can live a simple and happy life. Because the country has not been industrialized, we still have time to avoid ruin in the direction of total industrialization.

For now, of course, the situation makes it impossible to think realistically of communities, unless one thinks also of resistance. Could you say something about the meaning of that expression—"communities of resistance"?

Berrigan: I think the word *resistance* became very important around 1967 in the States. People were saying that it was necessary to take a step beyond protest. We could no longer look upon our style of life as merely being an occasion for this or that action. People had to begin thinking much more seriously and deeply about a long-term struggle in which they would stand up more visibly and perhaps with more risk. Of course, people saw that transition in quite a different way. Some of the political activists said that a moral, individual action was no longer enough; there must be unity of effort which was more and more highly political. One person refusing induction or going on trial or leaving the university would have no impact. Now there must be a community behind him.

Resistance, of course, was as ambiguous as the people who engaged in it. Some saw it as a violent word, some as nonviolent. I never heard the phrase "communities of resistance," as such, until around 1970; the word *resistance* around 1967 or 1968. But the idea developed that there would be communities, each member of which was dedicated to some violent or nonviolent ideal, some political or spiritual ideal, or some combination of these—political and spiritual.

I think it just to say that the roots of all this were among the religious people. I think they saw it first. Actually around that time, mainly as a result of Catonsville and the draft board actions, people began to say that it was not enough to perform one action and disperse. People had to stay together preparing for trial, talking around the country, preparing legal defense, raising money, educating other people. So the term arose out of those days after Catonsville. Communities of resistance were now required. I don't think a better term has been thought of.

Nhat Hanh: I think that's a very meaningful term. And *resistance*, at root, I think, must mean more than resistance against war. It is a resistance against all kinds of things that are like war. Because living in modern society, one feels that he cannot easily retain integrity, wholeness. One is robbed permanently of humanness, the capacity of being oneself. When I drive through Paris, the noises and the traffic jams make me nervous. Once I have gone through Paris I become less than myself. And there are so many things like that in modern life that make you lose yourself. So perhaps, first of all, resistance means opposition to being invaded, occupied, assaulted, and destroyed by the system. The purpose of resistance, here, is to seek the healing of yourself in order to be able to see clearly. This may sound as though it falls short of a positive act of resistance. Nevertheless, it's very basic.

I think that communities of resistance should be places where people can return to themselves more easily, where the conditions are such that they can heal themselves and recover their wholeness.

Berrigan: Something to do with occupation and invasion. The New Testament refers to "possession," the possession of people by demons. A very powerful action of Jesus is the casting out of demons. And one of the meanings of Christian sanctuary is a place where the demons are not welcome. Once you pass into these precincts, you're free from the influence of the demonic and the possession by machinery and pseudo-values and hatred.

But I was thinking, too, that when Jesus cast out the demons, He often entered into conversation with the people about what this might mean—whether they were conscious of being possessed. He was, I think, trying to determine the exact power of the demon over this person, the degree of self-possession which the person still retained. And it was only afterward in many cases, I think, that this tactic of His was understood by those who either read the account or were present during the event.

Psychiatric theories tend to throw out exorcism as being a primitive form of magic, something we have outgrown. In fact, there is a profound lesson here about the possession, the invasion, the loss of soul, loss of self-understanding on the part of many modern people. In the form almost of madness, one is invaded by the demonic values of this world, and runs with them.

Then the Book of Revelation extends all of that and says you don't really understand as long as you think it is only the person who is invaded. We must also see that there is an invasion of institutions and that the believing community is a charmed circle that withstands invasion. It is not an institution. First of all, it is a community; and secondly, this community lives by values which are utterly foreign to the values some men and women are possessed by. Thus, this community lives without attachment to money and prestige and hatred and violence and war. Its house will be buffeted and struck by the blows of the world; it can't exist in Nirvana in the sense of cheap grace. It has to earn its salvation by its love of the dispossessing Lord.

Nhat Hanh: The church was first founded, I think, as a community of resistance.

Berrigan: I think so.

Nhat Hanh: Yes. But finally, it couldn't resist and was invaded and possessed, and that is why new communities of resistance have to begin again.

A pagoda, a temple, a church, is built in a way that when you enter you recover yourself; you come into contact with the absolute reality, with God, with Buddha, with Buddhahood. And that is why the recovering of self is seen in architecture, in decorative art, in sacred music, in many things like that. So that when you come to the church or the temple you are helped by these things to return to yourself. I think that our communities of resistance should be built like a church or a temple where everything you see expresses the tendency to be oneself, to go back to oneself, to come into communion with reality. I believe that if that basic step is realized, then the second and third steps of resistance can be realized.

I look for communities of resistance—beautiful, healing, refreshing both in surroundings and in substance. In such communities you meet people who symbolize a kind of freshness; their look, their smile, their understanding, should be able to help. That is why a requirement of a community of resistance is the presence of at least one person who can offer that kind of atmosphere. Because of him or her you want to go back. I suggest that a community like that should, if possible, arise in a place that has pleasant surroundings. And there should be someone there in residence, so that when people think of him or her they feel some encouragement, some hope. The place should be identified with such a person. So even if that person is not there, when people come near the place, they would like to drop in. Because they know that person has been sitting under that tree. When I come and sit under that tree I feel the presence of a friend.

I'm not saying that a movement should be built on one person. But I think that if you want two persons, you should have one person first. A small brother always has need of a big brother during a certain period of time. I say this out of my own experience.

Berrigan: There are things, I think, peculiar to America which are very difficult to cope with, and which I don't think are experienced here in Paris, much less in Vietnam. There is the hyperconsciousness of young Americans about elitism which makes for a very uneasy relationship with someone who's older, especially someone who is famous or a media person—even though this person may resist all that. I think young people uneasily oscillate between admiration for a person like that and great distrust of him. This makes the situation on both sides very uneasy. It is difficult to be yourself because the media are invading, claiming one. It becomes a great source of difficulty to identify in a genuine fashion with a community of young people if you're trying to remain true to the struggle. At the same time, one is not at their stage of things because one is older and better known and is trying to be faithful to many different tasks. It would be easier if one chose, say, either of two things: I'm just going to travel and talk and write; or I'm just going to forget all that and stay with one community. But neither of these, I think, is a good solution. Somehow you find some uneasy way of being faithful to both aspects: people who ask you to go elsewhere, and the community that asks you to work at home. It's complex.

Nhat Hanh: I think all of us should overcome that kind of prejudice about people: leadership, fame, authority, prestige. Because none of that is important. Once I met a young student who sat with me for a while but didn't say anything. I began a conversation; he said, "It's so difficult to talk to you because you are well-known." I said, "I think that's silly, and it's your fault. It's not my fault because it's not my intention to sit far away from you." If you sit near a person and you find some pleasant feeling, that's good; you don't need anything more. The pleasant feeling and the communication that you establish—that's all you need.

Berrigan: What became of your community in Vietnam? Where are those members now?

Nhat Hanh: All scattered. Everyone still remembers the community, though the community is no longer there because of the war. But the task was, and is, a big one; many of us, thanks to it, have had occasion to be healed. Our wounds were very, very deep before we created the community. We established ourselves far away from the village, on a mountain in the deep forest. And we spent years there in order to heal ourselves. Because we were together, we created a kind of relationship that still exists to this day, even though we are scattered all over Vietnam and, in the case of Phuong and myself, exiled overseas. Everyone is still trying to do his best, but more or less in the same direction; and we feel the presence of each other.

That was only the first step of a community of resistance; the community of resistance should go beyond. The things Philip and Elizabeth and their friends are doing show other aspects of such communities. What I am thinking just now is that the two aspects we just discussed should complete each other, should help each other. It's our task to try to set up communities which are expressing life, reality, and are doing active resistance work.

Berrigan: I think so, yes. Too bad the monasteries, at least in Europe and the United States, don't see their task in this way. The trouble is that monasteries have become pleasant places where discipline and prayer go on, but where resistance does not go on. So today there is practically no conception of a monk or a nun who is a resisting person. In the States one has to say, though, that the nuns have moved remarkably in this direction, but usually against the understanding of their orders. The men have not followed this to any degree. I must say even with Merton it was a struggle to convince him that it was possible to be a monk in a way which was also actively resisting. He was in and out of that idea for many, many years, right up to his death. But the monks who will carry that idea forward—I don't know if they even exist.

Nhat Hanh: If in many monastic communities people are praying and meditating but do not resist, maybe it's because they do not pray and meditate properly. Because, I think, the object of praying and meditating is life—life in the most beautiful, glorious meaning of the word. The existence of Buddhism, of Christianity, and other religious disciplines has to do with life, with reality. When someone says that belief in Jesus is life, what life is he thinking of? The same kind of life that Jesus lived; it is the life which He suffered. So, meditating and praying should be in the context of life. And if you isolate yourself from the reality of suffering, I think that something is wrong.

Suppose there is a Buddhist temple in a village. The temple is not bombed, but the whole village has been bombed. People cry and weep and run about; the monks pray and meditate because the pagoda has not been bombed. I don't think such a situation can exist. I think the monks will both meditate and help a child who is wounded or meditate and help carry a wounded citizen out of the war zone, at the same time.

Berrigan: One would think in the right order of things that the monks would be the first to understand an historical situation which is morally intolerable—a war, above all else. That their discipline, their prayer, would render them acutely aware of what is occurring and intuitive about what to do. But this seems to be almost never verified. At least in my country the monks, except for very, very few, were among the last to come to any real understanding of things. They were the ones, in a sense, who resisted the resistance because they stood on their platonic trust in prayer as such, Mass as such, or divine office and chant as such, apart from any human intervention. They're always expecting God to intervene without their own intervention. The suppositions are very disturbing: real estate, land, buildings, remain untouched, undisturbed, uninvaded by suffering. The monks see themselves as men who pray in order that others do something. They pray in order that others "do God's will," as they say, that others suffer well, or others bear with prison. But the idea that their lives will be ground up is something very, very rare. And the realization that such a view of life is disincarnate, a betrayal of any real understanding of Christianity—that is very slow in coming.

Nhat Hanh: I mentioned the case of a bombed village. Not only should the monks have been aware of the suffering after the village was bombed, but even before. The resistance should have started before the bombing. The community of resistance is not only to back up the people who resist, to back them up in some kind of political way. It is a kind of fortress. Excuse me for using this word! I'm thinking of a fortress for resistance; because of the threat of being invaded, one has to resist.

Berrigan: I like the idea of the two aspects of the community. When I was in Ireland I saw a few of the towers the monks raised at the time of invasions in the ninth and tenth centuries. Once I walked in the country and came on one of these great circular towers on a hill and saw, around it, the ruins of a monastery.

The monks built these towers during the Dark Ages so that something could be saved. When the northern barbarians came down, driving everyone before them, burning and raping and destroying, the monks went into the tower. I remember standing inside this tower, this incredible building that stood for nine centuries and withstood successive waves of destruction and barbarism. The monks felt they should save something. They saved the people from the countryside; they lived in those towers for months. And they took with them (the historians say) two things: the books and the sacred vessels. The books symbolized the tradition, the story of their past, where they came from, who they were; and the vessels were the mystery, the Eucharist. Another way of saying who they were, that trust could not be broken, keeping the command of Christ—do this, do this, keep this going, don't allow this to be destroyed. And then when the worst was over, they came out again.

Everything else was gone, except love! Obviously one doesn't continue to resist unless one has a vision; it's ridiculous to think so. If one has only politics to resist politics, then everything goes! If one has an ideology to resist an ideology, everything goes. What is required to resist the barbarian is a vision, a tradition, a faith; everything else goes except the people, the community, the symbols of salvation.

After a great deal of ignorance on my part, mistakes, getting nowhere with community, I like Bonhoeffer's statement that the community is a gift and that in certain circumstances community will not happen. It's not a question of blaming anybody; it is very mysterious. But I don't think you can make a community happen.

You know, when I came out of jail, I was invited to teach at a seminary in New York. This was an interesting place, with Protestants and Catholics together. Much work had gone into creating this ecumenical arrangement where the Jesuits and Protestants would teach together and learn together. After a while, the superiors in Rome became uneasy about certain aspects of the community; so they unexpectedly ordered the place closed. And this was our best seminary in the country. As a result, there was a great sense of betrayal, a sense of alienation and shock.

I thought that here was a stroke of lightning in the darkness, where suddenly you see the real structure of something. If a tree is hit by lightning, it flares up and you see things you hadn't seen before. What I saw was that this community was not a community at all; after the shock wore off, everyone began making other plans—where we should go to teach, where we should go to study. Suddenly it was all over—something that people had worked for years to create.

And I saw that we were just like Cornell University; we were an arrangement of convenience among professional people to do a certain job. Once that job was interrupted or made impossible or finished, people moved on. But there were no human roots there, and whatever pain arose was felt for reasons that were quite peripheral to the main issue, which I thought was, Do we really have a kind of organic happening here? Have people found something profound about worship, about common faith, about stewardship, sharing, service? Is this something so precious that people are not going to have it destroyed automatically by some command from above? When I saw there was no response of that kind at all, it was very painful. I felt that if this thing can be brought down so quickly and easily, it cannot be what I thought it was. And one must try again, try elsewhere. But that was a very painful awakening.

Nhat Hanh: Sometimes a hasty judgment might lead you to cut off a relationship with a person. So, in my tradition we are taught to look at a tree or something like that for a long time. At first you don't know what use it is to look at a tree like that. You have to look until you can truly see it. And one day the tree reveals itself to you as a very substantial, real identity. It is not that you have a new tree or that the weather is better so that you can see the tree clearly, but something in oneself has changed so there is a new kind of relationship between you and the tree. Whether we can see the tree or not depends on us. Whether the tree can exist there or not depends on us. And whether one can be sad or sorrowful or joyful depends on the tree. So, a kind of wonderment arises. When I think of the relationship between two human beings, it's like that. It's not because you have some education that you can recognize a human being in his various aspects. You have to be with him and be with him a lot, and with a kind of open attitude, a kind of continuous self-transformation in you before such a relationship is possible, is fully realized.

I think that the encounter between man and God, the encounter between man and Buddhahood, reality, absolute reality, must be realized in the same way. It is not that the Buddha is more important than the tree. If you cannot have that kind of relationship with a tree, how can you expect to have it with the Buddha, with God, with ultimate reality?

I think that my contribution to the building of community life is to say, Do not judge each other too easily, too quickly, in terms of ideology, of point of view, strategies, things like that. Try to see the real person, the one with whom you live. You might discover aspects that will enrich you. It's like a tree that can shelter you.

But talking concretely, do you think that in countries like the United States it is still possible to create such communities? First, from the point of view of material needs, is it possible to set up the needed environment? And is it possible for a community living in that environment to produce what they need without having to rely too much on the outside? I ask you about the material aspect of building communities because we think it is still possible, in underdeveloped countries like ours, to build simple communities in which people live a simple life. Certainly this is possible in our south; because it's not cold, we can build very simple houses and wear simple clothes. And we can grow vegetables all year; there's no winter.

Berrigan: I don't think that the material question has ever been a very important one. In my experience, these communities can make it. If their sense of sacrifice and love of the community is alive, people always find ways of getting part-time work in a big city. You can work a few hours a day or some hours a week and be free; and then contribute that money to the others. There are friends who help, and there are cheap ways of living. Our failure has had nothing to do with material conditions. It's because we didn't have the guts or the heart to stay together to do serious work. One devastating difficulty is the mobility and pace which simply break people apart in the big cities, keep them from realizing and responding to the serious needs of others. I've never heard of any community that failed because it lacked material resources. Communities fail because they lack imagination and spiritual contact and soul and a sense of others and staying power and courage to move together and to live together.

Nhat Hanh: I notice in a number of communities there are persons who are not very active. They don't lead at all. But because they are there, others like to go there. And these people are not talented or well-known; they are just very refreshing, very human. I think we need such people in each community.

Berrigan: Oh, absolutely. All this is part of the refreshing variety that is so required. We have in the States a few people who have actually become clowns. They have learned how to juggle, mime, do acrobatics and all kinds of things just in order to be with communities which are overwhelmed with serious work and ideology. They come and go with these communities. It's a very great help. I think that without a sense of humor, without laughter and jokes and a good time among themselves, people go insane. That was always the big thing in prison—being able to play the guitar, write poetry, recite poetry, and, in general, show that life was not sour.

But I was hoping we could say something also about the place of the family in these communities. If married people are part of this, marriage also would be an expression of resistance. In fact, the image of the family, it seems to me, should be the same as the image of the community of resistance. The community is a family of resistance which goes beyond blood into friendship.

Nhat Hanh: And the existence of children is so refreshing and inspiring—the sight of a tiny baby, of very young children. One day I saw children playing; I felt so glad, so pleasant, I wrote Thomas Merton and said I hoped that he had time to watch children playing. He said, "Yes, you are right. Children are beautiful."

Berrigan: Is it true that in Vietnam the families have been part of the nonviolent resistance?

Nhat Hanh: Yes. Our community had all types of people—there were monks, writers, artists, and, from time to time, families came and stayed for weeks and months. In the Buddhist tradition there are two types of people who are responsible for the continuation of the church. One consists of those who live a contemplative life and stay in monasteries. After a period in monasteries, they find other places where they set up their own communities of learning and practice. Then there are those who take care of the task of preaching and doing other kinds of work related to the church. There is a close relationship between these two. We have been trying to set up communities in which married and unmarried can be together, to abolish the separation between the two. Like the order we founded about ten years ago. Monastic people and married people observe the same discipline and share the same life in the community. And I notice that this arrangement is more relaxing; no discrimination, no complex of superiority or authority.

Berrigan: Did this order begin because of the war situation and its needs?

Nhat Hanh: It was motivated by the need to actualize Buddhism, for Buddhism to be in the world, for the world; many such communities have arisen, to be of service in resistance. We notice in the order that living together and having time for meditation and sharing our feeling and experience—all this helped very much. If one was prevented from being with the community for a rather long time, he felt poorer for his absence; he could not perform his tasks as well as when he was together with his friends. It was so important; one's capacity to resist or to work was lessened very much by the lack of community life. Also one's faith was diminished.

Berrigan: Has any of these communities remained intact?

Nhat Hanh: Well, everything has been hurt by the war. The most important and the biggest obstacle we encounter is the instability. In the village of Tra Lôc in Quang Tri, we went to live with the peasants. We settled there and helped them with our experiences in community building. We built quite a beautiful village. We called it a pilot village. Then it was destroyed. We built a second time, and it was destroyed a second time. Now they are trying to rebuild it again. Well, many people say, "Why do you build again and again? Go to other, more stable places." But the fact is that if we give up it is a very serious blow to us and our friends there, the peasants.

Berrigan: It sounds like the work of community itself: always being destroyed, always starting again. And the instability that you speak of doesn't strike us in the same way in the States; no villages or cities are bombed. It strikes people; people are bombed in their heads. People are so isolated and disrupted by the conditions of life that they cannot stay together. It's just as though their whole landscape were wiped out. Spiritually, if not physically, it becomes very difficult to continue. I think this is part of the trauma that we spoke of earlier, another form of the damage which continues to destroy people.

Nhat Hanh: Do you think that it would be interesting to discuss the role of the community vis-à-vis personal religious experience? In other words, is it possible for an individual to find a way alone, to grow in his spiritual life?

Berrigan: It seems to me these are some of the most important questions facing us: just what resources are available, what discipline is required, and how people may come upon alternative ways of living today.

Nhat Hanh: There is a feeling among people that they are incomplete if they are not with each other.

Berrigan: I think that feeling is everywhere. There is a terrifying and destructive loneliness, especially in the cities—people trying to make it alone, or merely touching the periphery of one another's lives. And there is a vacuum at the center of their existence. That certainly is experienced by those who have no community roots. But whether or not a destructive loneliness can lead to a better direction is a very difficult question. Loneliness itself, a kind of psychic amputation from others, does not imply that one is ready for the discipline of a community. In fact, it might imply just the opposite. I think it's very necessary to help and encourage a person to realize that certain things must be lost, certain ways given up, and certain attitudes confronted. This is a great purification which all are not capable of. In the kibbutz we visited near Tel Aviv, we asked, "Why do people leave the kibbutz, and why do people come?" The leader said, "Well, they come because they're lonely, and they leave because they're lonely." And we said, "Well what does that mean? How can they be lonely with three hundred people around them?" He explained, "They have never found a way of sharing their existence even while they're here." A certain common religious tradition is a very great help. That's why monks and nuns, it seems to me, should be natural initiators and helpers in forming communities; they themselves have undergone this discipline.

Nhat Hanh: There is one resettlement village in Vietnam in which there are only three Catholic families, and the other 250 are Buddhist. But these Catholic families feel at home; they don't feel lonely. Maybe it is not necessary that all share the same religious ideals. What is important is that you find yourself in a situation where nobody discriminates. I think religions ought not separate people. (Yet there should be the particularity, the identity, of each group or each person.)

Berrigan: Of course we've seen instances where religion divides more than unites. This is an aspect of religion that should be reformed.

Nhat Hanh: And even in a community where everyone professes the same social pattern, the same social aim, there is division.

Berrigan: Why? Is it because the disciplines they share are outmoded? Or because individual characters are so different they cannot fuse?

Nhat Hanh: Of course there are many, many reasons, but there must be something that makes it more difficult now to live together than in the past. It may be that in the past, people had a feeling that they were already sure of their way. The way was there; for them it was only thinking of that way, advancing on that way. But in our time, the way has been very unclear, has required much searching.

Berrigan: When we became novices, for instance, there was a supposition shared by all who came into the order. You came to receive a common vision, accepted by everyone. It was a matter of great pride and esteem to be a member of this order. And for many years you were to be trained, judged, evaluated. But there was a vision underlying it. I think everyone came in with a common expectation of the way life would go. You were going later to be part of this or that community doing this or that work—writing or teaching or abroad in mission work. It was all clearly defined, and the communities you went into also had their own character, which you were invited to share, to be initiated into. But it was only rarely that you were asked to initiate something new.

Then suddenly, about fifteen years ago, all of that changed. The common assumptions of the community collapsed, more or less. The younger people began to question deeply, began to leave, refused to be part of these old institutions. They demanded smaller communities and new work and much more of the responsibility for their own community. They asked to create as they went, rather than merely to inherit and take along this baggage. And that, of course, has been catastrophic for many people, especially for older people.

I think that in my order the present difficulty is twofold. Many give up and wander off into a culture which is not capable of satisfying their needs. Or, those who stay often settle for a kind of arrangement of convenience. They live together peaceably and do professional work, but there's nothing very deep or humanly attractive about their fraternity.

Nhat Hanh: Remember the time you told me about a friend in Hanoi who said he could identify the Catholics by the look in their eyes? I think those believers belong to the period of time when people had no doubt concerning the way that had been prescribed. It is not very easy to find people like that in our times.

I have meditated on these problems, and I have seen that the notion of the *way* is very misleading. Most people think a way presupposes a distance and is like a rope linking one to a point in space, in time. Between two points, there is a distance and a link. When we detect a way to arrive at our destination, it is as though we made reservations on a flight.

But it is commonly thought that we remain the same, here and there. That is not the case, I believe. Because if you are not transformed on the way, you remain at the point of departure all the time; you never arrive at the destination. So, the way must be *in you;* the destination also must be in you and not somewhere else in space or time. If that kind of self-transformation is being realized in you, you *will* arrive. But if you remain the same, no plane can bring you to the point of arrival.

In the old time, in times when they were too sure of the way, people believed that there was a prescribed formula, a prescribed way. You only engaged in it, believed it, took the risk of belief, and you were transported along. In saying this, I'm not denying that man has to take the Law into account, that he has to rely on God, on Buddha. That is not the problem I'm talking about here. I'm thinking only of the misleading nature of the word *way,* which implies a destination. And it also implies the rejection of something and the embrace of something else. To me, that difference doesn't exist. The difference is merely a way of looking at this world. In Buddhist terms this very world in Nirvana; it depends on you. The way is in your mind; it is your way.

I want to express my hope in the community of people who have the same concerns and who are working for the same goals. What helps individuals in the community is your doing the same things I do, in your own way. I can learn from you. I feel the need of your presence. Not only because I have a feeling of physical loneliness, but I feel that I need you in many other respects: sharing of experiences, the support of each other in difficult moments (difficult moments not only understood as financial or political difficulties). Difficulties here might be purely in spiritual or religious terms, because in the life of a man who lives his religion, there are crises, and these crises are not only destructive, but very constructive, to destroy in order to build. That process of destruction-creation brings us ahead in our process of self-realization. So, the friend is at your side, even if he does nothing for you during this period of crisis, even if he says nothing to comfort you. The way he looks at you is something you need. There was one time when I underwent a crisis, and with me there was only a cat to look at me; and that helped a lot.

Berrigan: I think most of the communities that are staying together have this view that you speak of, a particular view of the way. That was a great word of Jesus about Himself, "I am the way." And also in the Acts of the Apostles, the early Christians always spoke of their faith as "the way." I've often thought of the people who are on the way, all the people I met recently in the Middle East. I meditate on their lives, their attitudes as they spoke to us, and it seems to me it makes no sense to be on one's way and yet act as though one had arrived. At least to a degree, one should be as content about this stage as though it were the last stage. Perhaps even more important, one should contain within himself all the necessary purity and love which signalize the end.

Gandhi often spoke of making the means equivalent to the end, so that one would not do anything today that would disperse or distract or corrupt what one is trying to move toward. That is perhaps one way of putting the greatness of the saints and of those we admire, that their lives contain the end in the very movement toward it.

Nhat Hanh: Very deep and true. I think that "I am the way" is much, much better than a statement like "I know the way." See, "I am the way," the way is more than an asphalt surface.

Berrigan: Or more than a road map.

Nhat Hanh: A road map! But I would make a distinction between the "I" in the phrase spoken by Jesus and the "I" that people may think of. The "I" in His statement is much, much larger and closer; not closer, it is life itself, His life! "I am the way." His life, which *is* life, is the way. If you don't look, if you don't really look at His life, you cannot see the way. But if you only satisfy yourself with the name, with saying a name, even if that name is Jesus, it is not the life of Jesus. The way should be understood as Jesus Himself and not just a few notions one has concerning His appearance.

Berrigan: I remember the movie of Pasolini, *The Gospel of St. Matthew.* Jesus is always in motion; He teaches while He's walking with His friends. And He's always walking very quickly, never seated somewhere; He's walking, and speaking over His shoulder while they're trying to keep up with Him. I thought this was not just a striking way of showing the urgency of the truth; it went deeper than that. It was as though life itself is a forward movement of awareness, of consciousness, of love; and He's dramatizing this by moving. His life is a movement, and they can't remain static and hope to grasp what He is about. They cannot remain in comfort; they cannot remain in the past. It's as though He's a kind of spool which is unwinding; they're trying to grab it as it goes, but it's always going. Or He's a great fish that they've caught; and yet He's not caught and they have to keep trying to draw Him to them. The fishing line always keeps unwinding ahead of them, because He's still ahead of them, and because He contains the whole thing. Even though they can only take in part of it, they must keep moving to grasp even that part.

So much "sacred" art has snuffed out the spirit of Jesus. He sits there in heavenly rest, tossing them words which they accept passively. But in Pasolini's movie there's a kind of uneasy motion, an effort to hear, and maybe not to hear all of it. Maybe the wind carries part of it away; but they just have to keep moving in order to hear Him, for the teaching is not static. The same physical effort required to stay with Him on the road is required to stay with Him in spirit.

Nhat Hanh: The teaching is not static because it is not mere words; it is the reality of life. There are those who have neither the way nor the life. They try to impose on others what they believe to be the way, but it is only words that have no connection with real life, a real way.

Berrigan: I often thought, What a privilege Merton had in his community. It's something I never had—a group of brothers of all ages and of all degrees of understanding, to live with them over long, long periods of time. Even at the edge of it, as he often was, and dissatisfied with many aspects of it, it was still a great source of satisfaction for him, as well as a rare grace. I was going over some of his letters recently, before I came to Paris, and I had a new sense of the suffering the community caused him, especially in the repressive efforts of superiors to censor some of his writing. And yet, I think I learned not so much what the community did for him, but that his suffering, acceptance, and understanding helped him grow in stature. I remember, too, difficult periods in my own order, when I would open up freely to him. His word was always, "We must stay where we are. We must stay with our community, even though it's absurd, makes no sense, and causes great suffering." He felt that the times were so chaotic, and people so quickly destroyed, that it was important to stand firm. He helped me in that way many times.

I think in the sixties he went through some of the worst times I ever witnessed among my friends. Yet he kept a deep understanding of the vitality a human being draws from his brothers and sisters. I often think that in my order part of my responsibility is parallel to his own: to keep a strong appreciation of the community, especially when so many are tempted to give up.

There is something mysterious in the timing of people or in projects. When we were in prison, there was a strong community. And everyone said, "We must get together when we get out because the war is still on and there's still work to do." So when we were released, we tried, but it was a disaster. Suddenly, we found that we were very different. People were moving in other directions; people were forming other relationships. People who got along in jail were now very difficult toward one another. After less than a year, this community of ex-prisoners just broke up. But now we find through letters that some are quietly coming together in Washington. Maybe it took all that time, two years or more, for the real thing to happen. Maybe the real thing just continues to happen.

Jonathan Schell

from *The Fate of the Earth*

(1984)

In this book, I have not sought to define a political solution to the nuclear predicament—either to embark on the full-scale reëxamination of the foundations of political thought which must be undertaken if the world's political institutions are to be made consonant with the global reality in which they operate or to work out the practical steps by which mankind, acting for the first time in history as a single entity, can reorganize its political life. I have left to others those awesome, urgent tasks, which, imposed on us by history, constitute the political work of our age. Rather, I have attempted to examine the physical extent, the human significance, and the practical dimensions of the nuclear predicament in which the whole world now finds itself. This predicament is a sort of cage that has quietly grown up around the earth, imprisoning every person on it, and the demanding terms of the predicament—its durability, its global political sweep, its human totality—constitute the bars of that cage. However, if a description of the predicament, which is the greatest that mankind has ever faced, cannot in itself reveal to us how we can escape, it can, I believe, acquaint us with the magnitude and shape of the task that we have to address ourselves to. And it can summon us to action.

To begin a summary with the matter of war: By effectively removing the limits on human access to the forces of nature, the invention of nuclear weapons ruined war, which depended for its results, and therefore for its usefulness, on the exhaustion of the forces of one of the adversaries. War depended, above all, on the weakness of human powers, and when human powers came to exceed human and other earthly endurance—when man as master of nature grew mightier than man as a vulnerable, mortal part of nature—war was ruined. Since war was the means by which violence was fashioned into an instrument that was useful in political affairs, the ruin of war by nuclear weapons has brought about a divorce between violence and politics. I submit that this divorce, being based on irreversible progress in scientific knowledge, not only is final but must ultimately extend across the full range of political affairs, and that the task facing the species is to shape a world politics that does not rely on violence. This task falls into two parts—two aims. The first is to save the world from extinction by eliminating nuclear weapons from the earth. Just recently, on the occasion of his retirement, Admiral Hyman Rickover, who devoted a good part of his life to overseeing the development and construction of nuclear-powered, nuclear-missile-bearing submarines for the United States Navy, told a congressional committee that in his belief mankind was going to destroy itself with nuclear arms. He also said of his part in the nuclear buildup that he was "not proud" of it, and added that he would like to "sink" the ships that he had poured so much of his life into. And, indeed, what everyone is now called on to do is to sink all the ships, and also ground all the planes, and fill in all the missile silos, and dismantle all the warheads. The second aim, which alone can provide a sure foundation for the first, is to create a political means by which the world can arrive at the decisions that sovereign states previously arrived at through war. These two aims, which correspond to the aims mentioned earlier of preserving the existence of life and pursuing the various ends of life, are intimately connected. If, on the one hand, disarmament is not accompanied by a political solution, then every clash of will between nations will tempt them to pick up the instruments of violence again, and so lead the world back toward extinction. If, on the other hand, a political solution is not accompanied by complete disarmament, then the political decisions that are made will not be binding, for they will be subject to challenge by force. And if, as in our present world, there is neither a political solution nor disarmament, then the world will be held perpetually at the edge of doom, and every clash between nuclear powers will threaten to push it over the edge.

The significance of the first aim—disarmament—which, without being paradoxical, we can describe as a "strategic" aim, can be clarified if we extend to its logical conclusion the reasoning that underlies the doctrine of deterrence. At present, the world relies on nuclear weapons both to prevent the use of nuclear weapons and to regulate the behavior of nations; but let us go a step—a very large step—further, and suppose, for a moment, that the world had established a political means of making international decisions and thus had no further need for nuclear or any other weapons. In order for such a thing to happen, we may ask, would the doctrine of deterrence and the fears on which it is based have to evaporate in the warmth of global good will? They would not. On the contrary, fear of extinction would have to increase, and permeate life at a deeper level: until it was great enough to inspire the complete rearrangement of world politics. Indeed, only when the world has given up violence does Churchill's dictum that safety is the sturdy child of terror actually become true. (At present, as we have seen, it is not safety but sovereignty that is the sturdy child of terror.) Under the current deterrence doctrine, one might say, safety is only the frail, anemic child of terror, and the reason is precisely that the terror is not yet robust enough to produce a sturdy offspring. For we still deny it, look away from it, and fail to let it reach deep enough into our lives and determine our actions. If we felt the peril for what it is—an urgent threat to our whole human substance—we would let it become the organizing principle of our global collective existence: the foundation on which the world was built. Fear would no longer dictate particular decisions, such as whether or not the Soviet Union might place missiles in Cuba; rather, it would be a moving force behind the establishment of a new system by which every decision was made. And, having dictated the foundation of the system, it would stand guard over it forever after, guaranteeing that the species did not slide back toward anarchy and doom.

This development would be the logical final goal of the doctrine of nuclear deterrence. In the pre-nuclear world, the threat of war, backed up by the frequent practice of war, served as a deterrent to aggression. Today,

Jonathan Schell

the threat of extinction, unsupported, for obvious reasons, by practice but backed up by the existence of nuclear arms and the threat to use them, serves as the ultimate deterrent. Thus, in today's system the actual weapons have already retired halfway from their traditional military role. They are "psychological" weapons, whose purpose is not to be employed but to maintain a permanent state of mind—terror—in the adversary. Their target is someone's mind, and their end, if the system works, is to rust into powder in their silos. And our generals are already psychological soldiers—masters of the war game and of the computer terminal but not, fortunately, of the battlefield. In this cerebral world, strategy confronts strategy and scenario battles scenario, the better to keep any of them from ever actually unfolding. But we need to carry this trend further. We need to make the weapons *wholly* cerebral—not things that sit in a silo ready to be fired but merely a thought in our minds. We need to destroy them. Only then will the logical fallacy now at the heart of the deterrence doctrine be removed, for only then will the fear of extinction by nuclear arms be used for the sole purpose of preventing extinction, and not also for the pursuit of national political aims. In a perfected nuclear deterrence, the knowledge in a disarmed world that rearmament potentially means extinction would become the deterrent. Now, however, it would be not that each nuclear-armed country would deter its nuclear-armed adversary but that awareness of the peril of extinction would deter all mankind from reëmbarking on nuclear armament. All human beings would join in a defensive alliance, with nuclear weapons as their common enemy. But since that enemy could spring only from our own midst, deterrer and deterred would be one. We thus arrive at the basic strategic principle of life in a world in which the nuclear predicament has been resolved: *Knowledge is the deterrent.* The nuclear peril was born out of knowledge, and it must abide in knowledge. The knowledge in question would be, in the first place, the unlosable scientific knowledge that enables us to build the weapons and condemns us to live forever in a nuclear world. This knowledge is the inexpungible minimum presence that the nuclear peril will always have in the life of the world, no matter what measures we adopt. In the second place, the knowledge would be the full emotional, intellectual, spiritual, and visceral understanding of the meaning of extinction—above all, the meaning of the unborn generations to the living. Because extinction is the end of mankind, it can never be anything more than "knowledge" for us; we can never "experience" extinction. It is *this* knowledge—this horror at a murderous action taken against generations yet unborn, which exerts pressure at the center of our existence, and which is the whole reality of extinction insofar as it is given to us to experience it—that must become the deterrent.

In a disarmed world, we would not have eliminated the peril of human extinction from the human scene—it is not in our power to do so —but we would at least have pitted our whole strength against it. The inconsistency of threatening to perpetrate extinction in order to escape extinction would be removed. The nuclei of atoms would still contain vast energy, and we would still know how to extinguish ourselves by releasing that energy in chain reactions, but we would not be lifting a finger to do it. There would be no complicity in mass murder, no billions of dollars spent on the machinery of annihilation, no preparations to snuff out the future generations, no hair-raising lunges toward the abyss.

The "realistic" school of political thinking, on which the present system of deterrence is based, teaches that men, on the whole, pursue their own interests and act according to a law of fear. The "idealistic" school looks on the human ability to show regard for others as fundamental, and is based on what Gandhi called the law of love. (Whereas the difference between traditional military thinking and nuclear strategic thinking lies in the different factual premises that they start from, the difference between the "realistic" and the "idealistic" schools of political philosophy lies in different judgments regarding human nature.) Historically, a belief in the necessity of violence has been the hallmark of the credo of the "realist"; however, if one consistently and thoroughly applies the law of fear in nuclear times one is driven not to rely on violence but to banish it altogether. This comes about as the result not of any idealistic assumption but of a rigorous application to our times of the strictly "military" logic of traditional war. For today the only way to achieve genuine national defense for any nation is for all nations to give up violence together. However, if we had begun with Gandhi's law of love we would have arrived at exactly the same arrangement. For to one who believed in nonviolence in a pre-nuclear setting the peril of extinction obviously

Jonathan Schell

adds one more reason—and a tremendous one, transcending all others—for giving up violence. Moreover, in at least one respect the law of love proves to fit the facts of this peril better than the law of fear. The law of fear relies on the love of self. Through deterrence—in which anyone's pursuit of self-interest at the expense of others will touch off general ruin that will destroy him, too—this self-love is made use of to protect everyone. However, self-love—a narrow, though intense, love—cannot, as we have seen, extend its protection to the future generations, or even get them in view. They still do not have any selves whose fear of death could be pooled in the common fund of fear, and yet their lives are at stake in extinction. The deterrence doctrine is a transaction that is limited to living people—it leaves out of account the helpless, speechless unborn (while we can launch a first strike against them, they have no forces with which to retaliate)—and yet the fate of the future generations is at the heart of extinction, for their cancellation is what extinction is. Their lives are at stake, but their vote is not counted. Love, however, can reach them—can enable them to be. Love, a spiritual energy that the human heart can pit against the physical energy released from the heart of matter, can create, cherish, and safeguard what extinction would destroy and shut up in nothingness. But in fact there is no need, at least on the practical level, to choose between the law of fear and the law of love, because ultimately they lead to the same destination. It is no more realistic than it is idealistic to destroy the world.

In supposing for a moment that the world had found a political means of making international decisions, I made a very large supposition indeed—one that encompasses something close to the whole work of resolving the nuclear predicament, for, once a political solution has been found, disarmament becomes a merely technical matter, which should present no special difficulties. And yet simply to recognize that the task is at bottom political, and that only a political solution can prepare the way for full disarmament and real safety for the species, is in itself important. The recognition calls attention to the fact that disarmament in isolation from political change cannot proceed very far. It alerts us to the fact that when someone proposes, as President Carter did in his Inaugural Address, to aim at ridding the world of nuclear weapons, there is an immense obstacle that has to be faced and surmounted. For the world, in freeing itself of one burden, the peril of extinction, must inevitably shoulder another: it must assume full responsibility for settling human differences peacefully. Morever, this recognition forces us to acknowledge that nuclear disarmament cannot occur if conventional arms are left in place, since as long as nations defend themselves with arms of any kind they will be fully sovereign, and as long as they are fully sovereign they will be at liberty to build nuclear weapons if they so choose. And if we assume that wars do break out and some nations find themselves facing defeat in the conventional arena, then the reappearance of nuclear arms, which would prevent such defeat, becomes a strong likelihood. What nation, once having entrusted its fortunes to the force of arms, would permit itself to be conquered by an enemy when the means of driving him back, perhaps with a mere threat, was on hand? And how safe can the world be while nations threaten one another's existence with violence and retain for themselves the sovereign right to build whatever weapons they choose to build? This vision of an international life that in the military sphere is restricted to the pre-nuclear world while in the scientific realm it is in the nuclear world is, in fact, thoroughly implausible. If we are serious about nuclear disarmament—the minimum technical requirement for real safety from extinction—then we must accept conventional disarmament as well, and this means disarmament not just of nuclear powers but of all powers, for the present nuclear powers are hardly likely to throw away their conventional arms while non-nuclear powers hold on to theirs. But if we accept both nuclear and conventional disarmament, then we are speaking of revolutionizing the politics of the earth. The goals of the political revolution are defined by those of the nuclear revolution. We must lay down our arms, relinquish sovereignty, and found a political system for the peaceful settlement of international disputes.

The task we face is to find a means of political action that will permit human beings to pursue any end for the rest of time. We are asked to replace the mechanism by which political decisions, whatever they may be, are reached. In sum, the task is nothing less than to reinvent politics: to reinvent the world. However, extinction will not wait for us to reinvent the world. Evolution was slow to produce us, but our extinction will

Jonathan Schell

be swift; it will literally be over before we know it. We have to match swiftness with swiftness. Because everything we do and everything we are is in jeopardy, and because the peril is immediate and unremitting, every person is the right person to act and every moment is the right moment to begin, starting with the present moment. For nothing underscores our common humanity as strongly as the peril of extinction does; in fact, on a practical and political plane it establishes that common humanity. The purpose of action, though, is not to replace life with politics. The point is not to turn life into a scene of protest; life is the point.

Whatever the eventual shape of a world that has been reinvented for the sake of survival, the first, urgent, immediate step, which requires no deep thought or long reflection, is for each person to make known, visibly and unmistakably, his desire that the species survive. Extinction, being in its nature outside human experience, is invisible, but we, by rebelling against it, can indirectly make it visible. No one will ever witness extinction, so we must bear witness to it before the fact. And the place for the rebellion to start is in our daily lives. We can each perform a turnabout right where we are—let our daily business drop from our hands for a while, so that we can turn our attention to securing the foundation of all life, out of which our daily business grows and in which it finds its justification. This disruption of our lives will be a preventive disruption, for we will be hoping through the temporary suspension of our daily life to ward off the eternal suspension of it in extinction. And this turnabout in the first instance can be as simple as a phone call to a friend, a meeting in the community.

However, even as the first steps are taken, the broad ultimate requirements of survival must be recognized and stated clearly. If they are not, we might sink into self-deception, imagining that inadequate measures would suffice to save us. I would suggest that the ultimate requirements are in essence the two that I have mentioned: global disarmament, both nuclear and conventional, and the invention of political means by which the world can peacefully settle the issues that throughout history it has settled by war. Thus, the first steps and the ultimate requirements are clear. If a busload of people is speeding down a mountainside toward a cliff, the passengers do not convene a seminar to investigate the nature of their predicament; they see to it that the driver applies the brakes. Therefore, at a minimum, a freeze on the further deployment of nuclear weapons, participated in both by countries that now have them and by countries that do not yet have them, is called for. Even better would be a reduction in nuclear arms—for example, by cutting the arsenals of the superpowers in half, as George Kennan suggested recently. Simultaneously with disarmament, political steps of many kinds could be taken. For example, talks could be started among the nuclear powers with the aim of making sure that the world did not simply blunder into extinction by mistake; technical and political arrangements could be drawn up to reduce the likelihood of mechanical mistakes and misjudgments of the other side's intentions or actions in a time of crisis, and these would somewhat increase the world's security while the predicament was being tackled at a more fundamental level. For both superpowers—and, indeed, for all other powers—avoiding extinction is a common interest than which none can be greater. And since the existence of a common interest is the best foundation for negotiation, negotiations should have some chance of success. However, the existence of negotiations to reduce the nuclear peril would provide no reason for abandoning the pursuit of other things that one believed in, even those which might be at variance with the beliefs of one's negotiating partner. Thus, to give one contemporary example, there is no need, or excuse, for the United States not to take strong measures to oppose Soviet-sponsored repression in Poland just because it is engaged in disarmament talks with the Soviet Union. The world will not end if we suspend shipments of wheat to the Soviet Union. On the other hand, to break off those talks in an effort to help the Poles, who will be as extinct as anyone else if a holocaust comes about, would be self-defeating. To seek to "punish" the other side by breaking off those negotiations would be in reality self-punishment. All the limited aims of negotiation can be pursued in the short term without danger if only the ultimate goal is kept unswervingly in mind. But ordinary citizens must insist that all these things be done, or they will not be.

If action should be concerted, as it eventually must be, in a common political endeavor, reaching across national boundaries, then, just as the aim of the endeavor would be to hold the gates of life open to the future generations, so its method would be to hold its own gates open to every living person. But it should be borne in mind that even if every person in the world were to enlist, the endeavor would include only an infinitesimal fraction of the people of the dead and the unborn generations, and so it would need to act with the circumspection and modesty of a small minority. From its mission to preserve all generations, it would not seek to derive any rights to dictate to the generations on hand. It would not bend or break the rules of conduct essential to a decent political life, for it would recognize that once one started breaking rules in the name of survival no rule would go unbroken. Intellectually and philosophically, it would carry the principle of tolerance to the utmost extreme. It would attempt to be as open to new thoughts and feelings as it would be to the new generations that would think those thoughts and feel those feelings. Its underlying supposition about creeds and ideologies would be that whereas without mankind none can exist, with mankind all can exist. For while the events that might trigger a holocaust would probably be political, the consequences would be deeper than any politics or political aims, bringing ruin to the hopes and plans of capitalists and socialists, rightists and leftists, conservatives and liberals alike. Having as the source of its strength only the spontaneously offered support of the people of the earth, it would, in turn, respect each person's will, which is to say his liberty. Eventually, the popular will that it marshalled might be deployed as a check on the power of whatever political institutions were invented to replace war.

Since the goal would be a nonviolent world, the actions of this endeavor would be nonviolent. What Gandhi once said of the spirit of nonviolent action in general would be especially important to the spirit of these particular actions: "In the dictionary of nonviolent action, there is no such thing as an 'external enemy.'" With the world itself at stake, all differences would by definition be "internal" differences, to be resolved on the basis of respect for those with whom one disagreed. If our aim is to save humanity, we must respect the humanity of every person. For who would be the enemy? Certainly not the world's political leaders, who, though they now menace the earth with nuclear weapons, do so only with our permission, and even at our bidding. At least, this is true for the democracies. We do not know what the peoples of the totalitarian states, including the people of the Soviet Union, may want. They are locked in silence by their government. In these circumstances, public opinion in the free countries would have to represent public opinion in all countries, and would have to bring its pressure to bear, as best it could, on all governments.

At present, most of us do nothing. We look away. We remain calm. We are silent. We take refuge in the hope that the holocaust won't happen, and turn back to our individual concerns. We deny the truth that is all around us. Indifferent to the future of our kind, we grow indifferent to one another. We drift apart. We grow cold. We drowse our way toward the end of the world. But if once we shook off our lethargy and fatigue and began to act, the climate would change. Just as inertia produces despair—a despair often so deep that it does not even know itself as despair—arousal and action would give us access to hope, and life would start to mend: not just life in its entirety but daily life, every individual life. At that point, we would begin to withdraw from our role as both the victims and the perpetrators of mass murder. We would no longer be the destroyers of mankind but, rather, the gateway through which the future generations would enter the world. Then the passion and will that we need to save ourselves would flood into our lives. Then the walls of indifference, inertia, and coldness that now isolate each of us from others, and all of us from the past and future generations, would melt, like snow in spring. E. M. Forster told us, "Only connect!" Let us connect. Auden told us, "We must love one another or die." Let us love one another—in the present and across the divides of death and birth. Christ said, "I come not to judge the world but to save the world." Let us, also, not judge the world but save the world. By restoring our severed links with life, we will restore our own lives. Instead of stopping the course of time and cutting off the human future, we would make it possible for the future generations to be born. Their inestimable gift to us, passed back from the future into the present, would be the wholeness and meaning of life.

Two paths lie before us. One leads to death, the other to life. If we choose the first path—if we numbly refuse to acknowledge the nearness of extinction, all the while increasing our preparations to bring it about—then we in effect become the allies of death, and in everything we do our attachment to life will weaken: our vision, blinded to the abyss that has opened at our feet, will dim and grow confused; our will, discouraged by the thought of trying to build on such a precarious foundation

Jonathan Schell

anything that is meant to last, will slacken; and we will sink into stupe-faction, as though we were gradually weaning ourselves from life in preparation for the end. On the other hand, if we reject our doom, and bend our efforts toward survival—if we arouse ourselves to the peril and act to forestall it, making ourselves the allies of life—then the anesthetic fog will lift: our vision, no longer straining not to see the obvious, will sharpen; our will, finding secure ground to build on, will be restored; and we will take full and clear possession of life again. One day—and it is hard to believe that it will not be soon—we will make our choice. Either we will sink into the final coma and end it all or, as I trust and believe, we will awaken to the truth of our peril, a truth as great as life itself, and, like a person who has swallowed a lethal poison but shakes off his stupor at the last moment and vomits the poison up, we will break through the layers of our denials, put aside our fainthearted excuses, and rise up to cleanse the earth of nuclear weapons.

The Immorality of War: A Conversation

(1992)

Pauling: Nuclear war is the ultimate immorality. But the immorality of war is not limited to the use of nuclear weapons. As early as biblical times, noncombatants were killed off in warfare. After the walls of Jericho fell, for example, the Israelites slaughtered all the women and children in the city.

In later times, however, combat came to be generally limited to soldiers—mostly young men—although kings too were sometimes killed in battle. Even when nations were at war, women and children were generally safe. In the American Civil War, for instance, casualties were mostly soldiers. Some bombings occurred during World War I; but, in World War II, both the British and the Americans adopted a policy of bombing cities—for example, Amsterdam, Hamburg, and Dresden—thus destroying thousands of civilians. Such acts are highly immoral. It is shocking that the modern world still does not ban war as totally degenerate. In our age, not even victors benefit from war. This aspect of the struggle for peace deserves special emphasis.

Ikeda: I agree entirely. As weapons have grown more destructive and national states more confident of their sovereign rights, large-scale, indiscriminate slaughter has become a commonplace of war. A backward look at the development of modern warfare makes apparent the extent to which human beings have become subservient to the weapons they have created. To alter this situation, each individual must strive to attain wisdom and enlightenment. We must do all we can to hasten the arrival of the day when the enlightened commonality of the human race assumes the lead in the work of preserving peace. In this connection, your quotation in *No More War,* from the words of your good friend Professor George B. Kistiakowsky is highly pertinent:

There simply is not enough time left before the world explodes. Concentrate ... on organizing, with so many others who are of like mind, a mass movement for peace such as there has not been before.

Pauling: If they are not misled by false statements from politicians and authorities, the people will recognize the need for world peace and their own responsibilities in achieving it. The power of the people to set politicians on the right track has been demonstrated a number of times during recent decades. I believe that, in the near future, a mass movement for peace, as described by Dr. Kistiakowsky, will lead to very significant progress.

Ikeda: Often presented as ideal statesmen, the ancient Indian kings Ashoka (died 232 B.C. and Kanishka (possibly the first half of the second century) were both devout Buddhists. Their approach to governing was imbued with the spirit of Buddhist compassion. Virtual embodiments of this philosophy, the flourishing Buddhist cultures they built in their peaceful nations are outstanding in all human history.

Although wars among believers in different religions have undeniably taken high tolls in human lives, numerous religions have exerted themselves unstintingly in the name of world peace. What is your opinion of peace movements conducted by people of religious faith?

Pauling: As you say, religious wars in the past have taken great tolls in human life. Indeed, as events in India, the Middle East, and other regions show, they continue to do so. Although the struggle between rich, property-holding Protestants and poor, laboring Catholics in Northern Ireland has a primarily economic basis, religion too plays a part in it. Of course, Catholics and Protestants have fought for centuries in the British Isles and elsewhere.

A few religions have worked for world peace on the basis of absolute pacifism. But, even in the United States, the Protestants began to take a moderately active interest in such work only in the last decade or two.

As to my own evaluation of peace movements based on religion, in general, I think they are fine. But problems sometimes arise. For example, the American Quakers are active in the work for world peace but refuse to participate in meetings attended by communists. For this reason, they broke up a meeting the British convened at Oxford because representatives from the Soviet Union had been invited. My wife and I, who were attending the meeting, could not understand their attitude. We work with all peace organizations because we need them. But not all religious groups see eye to eye with this attitude.

Ikeda: Undeniably much human blood has been shed in the name of religion; and, sadly, some of the wounds caused by religious conflicts remain unhealed. A religion that fails to contribute to human happiness and peace is useless, worse, it is pernicious. This is why I have long insisted that, in considering their roles in society it is essential to divide religions into two groups: those that work for the sake of vested authority and those that work for the good of humanity in general.

The pattern prevailing in many religions is one in which human beings are subjected to the rule of a god or some other absolute authority. Under such circumstances, human beings become means in the name of religious authority; and their very lives are sometimes sacrificed. I witnessed something of the fearsome aspects religion can assume when I examined mounds of human remains at a site once occupied by offices of the Inquisition in Lima, Peru. Any religion that sacrifices human life in the name of its own authority is wicked.

Religions ought to recognize the good of humanity as both the source of their being and the goal of their actions. The sole valid reason for a religion to exist is to contribute to the well-being and peace of the human race. The religion to which my fellow believers and I devote ourselves exists solely for the sake of humanity.

The members of Soka Gakkai International are all good citizens of the one hundred and fifty nations in which they live. All of them work steadily and unflaggingly in the name of peace. Their goals are the happiness of humanity, the prosperity of the whole world, and the rejection of war and all forms of violence. For this reason, we are especially eager to do everything we can to eliminate nuclear arms.

The Dilemma of the Absolute Pacifist: A Conversation

(1992)

Pauling: I certainly would support a Buddhist drive for peace; but, as I have said, I support all peace movements, even those conducted by communists. But I have doubts about absolute pacifism. What are absolute pacifists to do in a world that is not populated by absolute pacifists? Would it be possible to pursue an absolutely pacifist course under another Adolph Hitler, who wanted to dominate the world and eliminate everyone except German Aryans?

During World War II, some of my students were pacifists. One of them, an idealist, a Jew, and a vegetarian, was imprisoned. Since the prison authorities refused to recognize his vegetarianism and insisted on serving him meat, he nearly starved. Once released from jail, he was almost imprisoned a second time for failing to register for the draft. At his second trial, the judge asked whether he believed in God. Although he may well have believed in God, he confused the issue by arguing with the judge over the definition of the term. Still, on this occasion, he managed to stay out of jail.

With the exception of cases like his, the United States authorities were lenient with conscientious objectors and allowed them to work off their military obligations at various tasks. One of my students worked in a California lumber camp with other conscientious objectors. Two or three others worked with me on war projects, but I had to convince them that our tasks were too remote from fighting the enemy to trouble their consciences.

A German friend, a gifted violinist, physicist, and mathematician, was a pacifist who nonetheless was at first inducted into the German army. For a while, he operated an antiaircraft battery—he wrote me saying he thanked God he never hit anything—but later was taken out of the army and assigned to a factory where he applied his knowledge of mechanical processes in improving operational efficiency.

In spite of his brilliance, he was not made a professor until he was sixty years old because the Nazis would not award professorship to anyone who was not a member of their party. Consequently, he had a hard time making a living. Nonetheless, unlike many much less fortunate individuals, he survived the war.

Ikeda: The problem of absolute pacifism is and always has been difficult. In both theory and practice, it is hard to draw a line clearly dividing right from wrong in connection with it. Although understandably a thoroughly confirmed, absolute pacifist might be willing to face death for his faith, the political efficacy of absolute pacifism is sometimes problematic. As you say, what good would an absolute pacifist be able to do under a Hitler-like regime?

We have already mentioned Einstein's predicament in feeling impelled by the Nazi threat to recommend to President Roosevelt that the United States go ahead with research leading to the production of the atomic bomb. He was a pacifist in a world not inhabited completely by fellow pacifists:

> *I was well aware of the dreadful danger which would threaten mankind were the experiments to prove successful. Yet I felt impelled to take the step because it seemed probable that the Germans might be working on the same problem with every prospect of success. I saw no alternative but to act as I did, although I have always been a convinced pacifist.* —Einstein on Peace

He was afraid of what might happen if the Nazis succeeded in the nuclear research he knew they were conducting at the time. He called himself a convinced, not an absolute, pacifist. Nonetheless, the following quotation from an apologia he published in Japanese newspapers after World War II suggests that absolute pacifism was his ideal.

> *Gandhi, the greatest political genius of our time, indicated the path to be taken. He gave proof of what sacrifice man is capable once he has discovered the right path. His work on behalf of India's liberation is living testimony to the fact that man's will, sustained by an indomitable conviction, is more powerful than material forces that seem insurmountable.* —Einstein on Peace

In the past, international relations have generally been controlled exclusively by diplomats and politicians. Today, however, sophisticated developments in technology and transportation have greatly altered the traditional arrangement. On one level, it has become more common for supreme leaders of national states to meet person to person. On another level, tourism and cultural and sports events greatly accelerate the pace at which ordinary peoples come to know and understand each other, thus putting a more generally human face on the way history is made. This is as it must be. Instead of allowing themselves to be led about by the noses at the beck and call of national states, the ordinary citizens must assume the principal role in history.

Before concluding our dialogue, I should like to touch briefly on Japan's role in the contemporary world. Although the Japanese people themselves may not always enjoy the fruits of national affluence as fully as they would like, Japan has become a great economic power and as such is expected by other nations to make suitable contributions to the management of the world. As the only nation ever to have suffered an atomic bombing, Japan certainly has a mission of contributing to the peace of the whole planet. Since you have visited Japan often and understand our nation well, your advice in this connection would be most welcome.

Pauling: Japan must continue refusing to rely on a large military force and refraining from developing nuclear weapons. In this way, Japan can be a leader in the drive for world peace. As a consequence of her rapid technological growth, Japan has become one of the most important nations. The health of the Japanese people has improved greatly in the last fifty years. For example, life expectancy has become much higher than it was in the Japan of the 1930s.

Japan has made a step in the direction of freeing the world of war by limiting its military establishment since the end of World War II. I realize that steps are being taken toward expanding the armed forces. But part of the prosperity of the nation in the past twenty-five years has been made possible by the absence of a great military drain (of the usual 10 or 20 percent of the gross national product) on the budget. I can see no reason for Japan to assume the burden of a large military force.

War Is Peace

(2001)

As darkness deepened over Afghanistan on Sunday, October 7, 2001, the U.S. government, backed by the International Coalition Against Terror (the new, amenable surrogate for the United Nations), launched air strikes against Afghanistan. TV channels lingered on computer-animated images of Cruise missiles, stealth bombers, Tomahawks, "bunker-busting" missiles and Mark 82 high-drag bombs. All over the world, little boys watched goggle-eyed and stopped clamouring for new video games.

The UN, reduced now to an ineffective abbreviation, wasn't even asked to mandate the air strikes. (As Madeleine Albright once said, "The US acts multilaterally when it can, and unilaterally when it must.") The "evidence" against the terrorists was shared amongst friends in the "Coalition." After conferring, they announced that it didn't matter whether or not the 'evidence' would stand up in a court of law. Thus, in an instant, were centuries of jurisprudence carelessly trashed.

Nothing can excuse or justify an act of terrorism, whether it is committed by religious fundamentalists, private militia, people's resistance movements—or whether it's dressed up as a war of retribution by a recognised government. The bombing of Afghanistan is not revenge for New York and Washington. It is yet another act of terror against the people of the world. Each innocent person that is killed must be added to, not set off against, the grisly toll of civilians who died in New York and Washington.

People rarely win wars, governments rarely lose them. People get killed. Governments moult and regroup, hydra-headed. They first use flags to shrink-wrap peoples' minds and suffocate real thought, and then as ceremonial shrouds to cloak the mangled corpses of the willing dead. On both sides, in Afghanistan as well as America, civilians are now hostage to the actions of their own governments. Unknowingly, ordinary people in both countries share a common bond—they have to live with the phenomenon of blind, unpredictable terror. Each batch of bombs that is dropped on Afghanistan is matched by a corresponding escalation of mass hysteria in America about anthrax, more hijackings and other terrorist acts.

There is no easy way out of the spiraling morass of terror and brutality that confronts the world today. It is time now for the human race to hold still, to delve into its wells of collective wisdom, both ancient and modern. What happened on September 11 changed the world forever. Freedom, progress, wealth, technology, war—these words have taken on new meaning. Governments have to acknowledge this transformation, and approach their new tasks with a modicum of honesty and humility. Unfortunately, up to now, there has been no sign of any introspection from the leaders of the International Coalition. Or the Taliban.

When he announced the air strikes, President George Bush said, "We're a peaceful nation." America's favourite ambassador, Tony Blair (who also holds the portfolio of Prime Minister of the UK), echoed him: "We're a peaceful people."

So now we know. Pigs are horses. Girls are boys. War is Peace.

Speaking at the FBI headquarters a few days later, President Bush said: "This is our calling. This is the calling of the United States of America. The most free nation in the world. A nation built on fundamental values that reject hate, reject violence, rejects murderers and rejects evil. We will not tire."

Here is a list of the countries that America has been at war with— and bombed—since World War II: China (1945–46, 1950–53); Korea (1950–53); Guatemala (1954, 1967–69); Indonesia (1958); Cuba (1959–

60); the Belgian Congo (1964); Peru (1965); Laos (1964–73); Vietnam (1961–73); Cambodia (1969–70); Grenada (1983); Libya (1986); El Salvador (1980s); Nicaragua (1980s); Panama (1989), Iraq (1991–99), Bosnia (1995), Sudan (1998); Yugoslavia (1999). And now Afghanistan.

Certainly it does not tire—this, the Most Free nation in the world. What freedoms does it uphold? Within its borders, the freedoms of speech, religion, thought; of artistic expression, food habits, sexual preferences (well, to some extent) and many other exemplary, wonderful things. Outside its borders, the freedom to dominate, humiliate and subjugate—usually in the service of America's real religion, the "free market." So when the US government christens a war "Operation Infinite Justice," or "Operation Enduring Freedom," we in the Third World feel more than a tremor of fear. Because we know that Infinite Justice for some means Infinite Injustice for others. And Enduring Freedom for some means Enduring Subjugation for others.

The International Coalition Against Terror is largely a cabal of the richest countries in the world. Between them, they manufacture and sell almost all of the world's weapons, they possess the largest stockpile of weapons of mass destruction—chemical, biological and nuclear. They have fought the most wars, account for most of the genocide, subjection, ethnic cleansing and human rights violations in modern history, and have sponsored, armed, and financed untold numbers of dictators and despots. Between them, they have worshipped, almost deified, the cult of violence and war. For all its appalling sins, the Taliban just isn't in the same league.

The Taliban was compounded in the crumbling crucible of rubble, heroin, and landmines in the backwash of the Cold War. Its oldest leaders are in their early 40s. Many of them are disfigured and handicapped, missing an eye, an arm or a leg. They grew up in a society scarred and devastated by war. Between the Soviet Union and America, over 20 years, about $45 billion worth of arms and ammunition was poured into Afghanistan. The latest weaponry was the only shard of modernity to intrude upon a thoroughly medieval society. Young boys—many of them orphans—who grew up in those times, had guns for toys, never knew the security and comfort of family life, never experienced the company of women. Now, as adults and rulers, the Taliban beat, stone, rape, and brutalise women; they don't seem to know what else to do with them. Years of war have stripped them of gentleness, inured them to kindness and human compassion. They dance to the percussive rhythms of bombs raining down around them. Now they've turned their monstrosity on their own people.

With all due respect to President Bush, the people of the world do not have to choose between the Taliban and the US government. All the beauty of human civilization—our art, our music, our literature—lies beyond these two fundamentalist, ideological poles. There is as little chance that the people of the world can all become middle-class consumers as there is that they'll all embrace any one particular religion. The issue is not about Good vs. Evil or Islam vs. Christianity as much as it is about space. About how to accommodate diversity, how to contain the impulse towards hegemony—every kind of hegemony, economic, military, linguistic, religious, and cultural. Any ecologist will tell you how dangerous and fragile a monoculture is. A hegemonic world is like having a government without a healthy opposition. It becomes a kind of dictatorship. It's like putting a plastic bag over the world, and preventing it from breathing. Eventually, it will be torn open.

One and a half million Afghan people lost their lives in the 20 years of conflict that preceded this new war. Afghanistan was reduced to rubble, and now, the rubble is being pounded into finer dust. By the second day of the air strikes, US pilots were returning to their bases without dropping their assigned payload of bombs. As one pilot put it, Afghanistan is "not a target-rich environment." At a press briefing at the Pentagon, Donald Rumsfeld, US defense secretary, was asked if America had run out of targets.

"First we're going to re-hit targets," he said, "and second, we're not running out of targets, Afghanistan is . . ." This was greeted with gales of laughter in the Briefing Room.

By the third day of the strikes, the US defense department boasted that it had "achieved air supremacy over Afghanistan." Did they mean that they had destroyed both, or maybe all 16, of Afghanistan's planes?)

On the ground in Afghanistan, the Northern Alliance—the Taliban's old enemy, and therefore the International Coalition's newest friend—is making headway in its push to capture Kabul. (For the archives, let it be said that the Northern Alliance's track record is not very different from the Taliban's. But for now, because it's inconvenient, that little detail is being glossed over.) The visible, moderate, "acceptable" leader of the Alliance, Ahmed Shah Masood, was killed in a suicide-bomb attack early in September. The rest of the Northern Alliance is a brittle confederation of brutal warlords, ex-communists, and unbending clerics. It is a disparate group divided along ethnic lines, some of whom have tasted power in Afghanistan in the past.

Until the US air strikes, the Northern Alliance controlled about 5 per cent of the geographical area of Afghanistan. Now, with the Coalition's help and "air cover," it is poised to topple the Taliban. Meanwhile, Taliban soldiers, sensing imminent defeat, have begun to defect to the Alliance. So the fighting forces are busy switching sides and changing uniforms. But in an enterprise as cynical as this one, it seems to matter hardly at all. Love is hate, north is south, peace is war.

Among the global powers, there is talk of "putting in a representative government." Or, on the other hand, of "restoring" the Kingdom to Afghanistan's 89-year-old former king, Zahir Shah, who has lived in exile in Rome since 1973. That's the way the game goes—support Saddam Hussein, then "take him out"; finance the mujahideen, then bomb them to smithereens; put in Zahir Shah and see if he's going to be a good boy. (Is it possible to "put in" a representative government? Can you place an order for Democracy—with extra cheese and jalapeno peppers?)

Reports have begun to trickle in about civilian casualties, about cities emptying out as Afghan civilians flock to the borders which have been closed. Main arterial roads have been blown up or sealed off. Those who have experience of working in Afghanistan say that by early November, food convoys will not be able to reach the millions of Afghans (7.5 million according to the UN) who run the very real risk of starving to death during the course of this winter. They say that in the days that are left before winter sets in, there can either be a war, or an attempt to reach food to the hungry. Not both.

As a gesture of humanitarian support, the US government airdropped 37,000 packets of emergency rations into Afghanistan. It says it plans to drop a total of 5,000,000 packets. That will still only add up to a single meal for half-a-million people out of the several million in dire need of food. Aid workers have condemned it as a cynical, dangerous, public-relations exercise. They say that air-dropping food packets is worse than futile. First, because the food will never get to those who really need it. More dangerously, those who run out to retrieve the packets risk being blown up by landmines. A tragic alms race.

Nevertheless, the food packets had a photo-op all to themselves. Their contents were listed in major newspapers. They were vegetarian, we're told, as per Muslim Dietary Law(!) Each yellow packet, decorated with the American flag, contained: rice, peanut butter, bean salad, strawberry jam, crackers, raisins, flat bread, an apple fruit bar, seasoning, matches, a set of plastic cutlery, a serviette and illustrated user instructions.

After three years of unremitting drought, an air-dropped airline meal in Jalalabad! The level of cultural ineptitude, the failure to understand what months of relentless hunger and grinding poverty really mean, the US government's attempt to use even this abject misery to boost its self-image, beggars description.

Reverse the scenario for a moment. Imagine if the Taliban government was to bomb New York City, saying all the while that its real target was the US government and its policies. And suppose, during breaks between the bombing, the Taliban dropped a few thousand packets containing nan and kababs impaled on an Afghan flag. Would the good people of New York ever find it in themselves to forgive the Afghan government? Even if they were hungry, even if they needed the food, even if they ate it, how would they ever forget the insult, the condescension? Rudy Giuliani, Mayor of New York City, returned a gift of $10 million from a Saudi prince because it came with a few words of friendly advice about American policy in the Middle East. Is pride a luxury only the rich are entitled to?

Far from stamping it out, igniting this kind of rage is what creates terrorism. Hate and retribution don't go back into the box once you've let them out. For every "terrorist" or his "supporter" that is killed, hundreds of innocent people are being killed too. And for every hundred innocent people killed, there is a good chance that several future terrorists will be created.

Where will it all lead?

Setting aside the rhetoric for a moment, consider the fact that the world has not yet found an acceptable definition of what "terrorism" is. One country's terrorist is too often another's freedom fighter. At the heart of the matter lies the world's deep-seated ambivalence towards violence. Once violence is accepted as a legitimate political instrument, then the morality and political acceptability of terrorists (insurgents or freedom fighters) becomes contentious, bumpy terrain. The US government itself has funded, armed, and sheltered plenty of rebels and insurgents around the world. The CIA and Pakistan's ISI trained and armed the mujahideen who, in the 1980s, were seen as terrorists by the government in Soviet-occupied Afghanistan. While President Reagan posed with them for a group portrait and called them the moral equivalents of America's founding fathers. Today, Pakistan—America's ally in this new war—sponsors insurgents who cross the border into Kashmir in India. Pakistan lauds them as "freedom fighters," India calls them "terrorists." India, for its part, denounces countries who sponsor and abet terrorism, but the Indian army has, in the past, trained separatist Tamil rebels asking for a homeland in Sri Lanka—the LTTE, responsible for countless acts of bloody terrorism. (Just as the CIA abandoned the mujahideen after they had served its purpose, India abruptly turned its back on the LTTE for a host of political reasons. It was an enraged LTTE suicide-bomber who assassinated former Indian prime minister Rajiv Gandhi in 1991.)

It is important for governments and politicians to understand that manipulating these huge, raging human feelings for their own narrow purposes may yield instant results, but eventually and inexorably, they have disastrous consequences. Igniting and exploiting religious sentiments for reasons of political expediency is the most dangerous legacy that governments or politicians can bequeath to any people—including their own. People who live in societies ravaged by religious or communal bigotry know that every religious text—from the Bible to the Bhagwad Gita—can be mined and misinterpreted to justify anything, from nuclear war to genocide to corporate globalisation.

This is not to suggest that the terrorists who perpetrated the outrage on September 11 should not be hunted down and brought to book. They must be. But is war the best way to track them down? Will burning the haystack find you the needle? Or will it escalate the anger and make the world a living hell for all of us?

At the end of the day, how many people can you spy on, how many bank accounts can you freeze, how many conversations can you eavesdrop on, how many e-mails can you intercept, how many letters can you open, how many phones can you tap? Even before September 11, the CIA had accumulated more information than is humanly possible to process. (Sometimes, too much data can actually hinder intelligence—small wonder the US spy satellites completely missed the preparation that preceded India's nuclear tests in 1998.)

The sheer scale of the surveillance will become a logistical, ethical and civil rights nightmare. It will drive everybody clean crazy. And freedom—that precious, precious thing—will be the first casualty. It's already hurt and hemorrhaging dangerously.

Governments across the world are cynically using the prevailing paranoia to promote their own interests. All kinds of unpredictable political forces are being unleashed. In India, for instance, members of the All India People's Resistance Forum, who were distributing anti-war and anti-US pamphlets in Delhi, have been jailed. Even the printer of the leaflets was arrested. The right-wing government (while it shelters Hindu extremist groups like the Vishwa Hindu Parishad and the Bajrang Dal) has banned the Students' Islamic Movement of India and is trying to revive an anti-terrorist act which had been withdrawn after the Human Rights Commission reported that it had been more abused than used. Millions of Indian citizens are Muslim. Can anything be gained by alienating them?

Every day that the war goes on, raging emotions are being let loose into the world. The international press has little or no independent access to the war zone. In any case, mainstream media, particularly in the US, has more or less rolled over, allowing itself to be tickled on the stomach with press hand-outs from militarymen and government officials. Afghan radio stations have been destroyed by the bombing. The Taliban has always been deeply suspicious of the Press. In the propaganda war, there is no accurate estimate of how many people have been killed, or how much destruction has taken place. In the absence of reliable information, wild rumours spread.

Put your ear to the ground in this part of the world, and you can hear the thrumming, the deadly drumbeat of burgeoning anger. Please. Please, stop the war now. Enough people have died. The smart missiles are just not smart enough. They're blowing up whole warehouses of suppressed fury.

President George Bush recently boasted: "When I take action, I'm not going to fire a $2 million missile at a $10 empty tent and hit a camel in the butt. It's going to be decisive." President Bush should know that there are no targets in Afghanistan that will give his missiles their money's worth. Perhaps, if only to balance his books, he should develop some cheaper missiles to use on cheaper targets and cheaper lives in the poor countries of the world. But then, that may not make good business sense to the Coalition's weapons manufacturers. It wouldn't make any sense at all, for example, to the Carlyle Group—described by the Industry Standard as "the world's largest private equity firm," with $12 billion under management. Carlyle invests in the defense sector and makes its money from military conflicts and weapons spending.

Carlyle is run by men with impeccable credentials. Former US defense secretary Frank Carlucci is Carlyle's chairman and managing director (he was a college roommate of Donald Rumsfeld's). Carlyle's other partners include former US secretary of state James A. Baker III, George Soros, Fred Malek (George Bush Sr.'s campaign manager). An American paper—the Baltimore *Chronicle and Sentinel*—says that former President George Bush Sr. is reported to be seeking investments for the Carlyle Group from Asian markets. He is reportedly paid not inconsiderable sums of money to make "presentations" to potential government-clients.

Ho Hum. As the tired saying goes, it's all in the family.

Then there's that other branch of traditional family business—oil. Remember, President George Bush (Jr.) and Vice-President Dick Cheney both made their fortunes working in the US oil industry.

Turkmenistan, which borders the northwest of Afghanistan, holds the world's third largest gas reserves and an estimated six billion barrels of oil reserves. Enough, experts say, to meet American energy needs for the next 30 years (or a developing country's energy requirements for a couple of centuries.) America has always viewed oil as a security consideration, and protected it by any means it deems necessary. Few of us doubt that its military presence in the Gulf has little to do with its concern for human rights and almost entirely to do with its strategic interest in oil.

Oil and gas from the Caspian region currently moves northward to European markets. Geographically and politically, Iran and Russia are major impediments to American interests. In 1998, Dick Cheney—then CEO of Halliburton, a major player in the oil industry—said: "I can't think of a time when we've had a region emerge as suddenly to become as strategically significant as the Caspian. It's almost as if the opportunities have arisen overnight." True enough.

For some years now, an American oil giant called Unocal has been negotiating with the Taliban for permission to construct an oil pipeline through Afghanistan to Pakistan and out to the Arabian Sea. From here, Unocal hopes to access the lucrative "emerging markets" in South and Southeast Asia. In December 1997, a delegation of Taliban mullahs traveled to America and even met US State Department officials and Unocal executives in Houston. At that time the Taliban's taste for public executions and its treatment of Afghan women were not made out to be the crimes against humanity that they are now. Over the next six months, pressure from hundreds of outraged American feminist groups was brought to bear on the Clinton administration. Fortunately, they managed to scuttle the deal. And now comes the US oil industry's big chance.

In America, the arms industry, the oil industry, the major media networks, and, indeed, US foreign policy, are all controlled by the same business combines. Therefore, it would be foolish to expect this talk of guns and oil and defense deals to get any real play in the media. In any case, to a distraught, confused people whose pride has just been wounded, whose loved ones have been tragically killed, whose anger is fresh and sharp, the inanities about the "Clash of Civilisations" and the "Good vs. Evil" discourse home in unerringly. They are cynically doled out by government spokesmen like a daily dose of vitamins or anti-depressants. Regular medication ensures that mainland America continues to remain the enigma it has always been—a curiously insular people, administered by a pathologically meddlesome, promiscuous government.

And what of the rest of us, the numb recipients of this onslaught of what we know to be preposterous propaganda? The daily consumers of the lies and brutality smeared in peanut butter and strawberry jam being air-dropped into our minds just like those yellow food packets. Shall we look away and eat because we're hungry, or shall we stare unblinking at the grim theatre unfolding in Afghanistan until we retch collectively and say, in one voice, that we have had enough?

As the first year of the new millennium rushes to a close, one wonders—have we forfeited our right to dream? Will we ever be able to re-imagine beauty? Will it be possible ever again to watch the slow, amazed blink of a new-born gecko in the sun, or whisper back to the marmot who has just whispered in your ear—without thinking of the World Trade Center and Afghanistan?

Arundhati Roy

Tim Wise

Who's Being Naïve? War-Time Realism through the Looking Glass

(2001)

To hear those who support the United States' air assault on Afghanistan tell it, those of us who doubt the likely efficacy of such a campaign, and who question its fundamental morality are not only insufficiently patriotic but dangerously naïve. Lampooning the left for adhering to such ostensibly simplistic slogans as "violence begets violence," these self-proclaimed pragmatists insist that sometimes force is necessary and that in the case of Osama bin Laden and al-Qaeda, little else could possibly serve to diminish the threat of terrorist attack.

It takes me back, all this self-assured confidence in the value of pre-emptive assault. To 1986 in particular, when a co-worker of mine insisted that although our bombing of Libya had failed to kill Colonel Quadafi, that by killing his daughter we had nonetheless served the cause of peace. After all, said my co-worker, she was destined to become a terrorist someday, so better to kill her before she grew. That others might be able to apply the same logic to Americans—who, after all *could* grow up to be Elliot Abrams—was lost on her, as she was convinced the world had been made safer that day.

Of course, just two years after my colleague insisted that our assault on Libya had made us safer, 259 people in a plane over Lockerbie, Scotland—and eleven more on the ground—learned how dangerously ignorant such faith really was. They, as it turned out, apparently became the victims of actual Libyan terrorists, enraged by the previous U.S. attack on their country.*

All this talk of what's naïve and what's realistic seems nothing if not bizarre: as if words no longer have their original meanings, or mean the opposite of what one might think.

So to be realistic means to believe that bombing one of the poorest nations on Earth will not only reduce terrorism, but also fail to ignite a new round of anti-American fanaticism. To be naïve, on the other hand, is to pay attention to modern history, which tells us that bombing people is rather likely to fuel their anger, resentment, and desire for revenge.

To be realistic is to think that pummeling one nation will have some appreciable effect on al-Qaeda, despite the fact that the group operates in sixty-four countries including many allies whom we have no intention of bombing. To be naïve is to point out that terrorists aren't reliant on one, or even several countries to operate, and as such, we could eradicate every member of the Taliban tomorrow without delaying by so much as a day any future attacks on our shores.

To be realistic is to say things like "all they respect is force." To be naïve is to point out that the force we have demonstrated over the years by our support for Israel, or bombing and sanctions against Iraq, has apparently led not to something so kind as their respect for us, but rather to their willingness to slaughter as many Americans as possible. If this is

---

* Although a Libyan was convicted for the bombing of the Pan Am flight over Scotland, and Libyan involvement has long been the accepted wisdom regarding this incident, there is another school of thought worth mentioning. It too would follow the logic of a revenge bombing and would make the point of this author's paragraph just the same. There are many who believe that the terrorists responsible for the Pan Am bombing were not Libyans, but rather Iranians, retaliating for the unprovoked shooting down of a civilian Iranian airbus by a U.S. Naval vessel earlier that same year (1988). As with the 1986 bombing of Libya, in the aftermath of this incident, I heard many people say it was probably for the best, because that would mean a few hundred less anti-American "fanatics" and potential terrorists down the line. George Bush Sr.—a presidential candidate at the time—remarked: "I will never apologize for the United States of America. I don't care what the facts are."

how al-Qaeda shows respect, I shudder to think what disdain must look like.

To be realistic is to say, "we tried peace and peace failed." To be naïve is to ask when, exactly, did the U.S. try peace: in the region, or specifically in Afghanistan? Was it when we were selling Stinger missiles to the Mujahadeen, so as to help them fight the Soviets? Or was it after, when we left the nation in ruins, unconcerned about helping rebuild so long as the Russians had fled? Or was it when we cozied up to the Taliban because they promised to crack down on opium cultivation, using the time-honored anti-crime techniques of extremist Islam?

To be realistic is to insist that nations harboring terrorists must be brought to justice. To be naïve is to note that a) we aren't really serious about that; after all, many nations that do so are coalition partners in the war on Afghanistan; and b) by that standard, any number of nations would have the right to attack us. Let us not forget that we have harbored and even taught terrorists and death squad leaders at the School of the Americas at Fort Benning, Georgia. We have harbored known Cuban terrorists in Miami. And we are still refusing to hand over Emanuel Constant to Haitian authorities, even though he has been found guilty in a court of law for involvement in the murder of over 4000 people in the early '90's coup attempt there.

To be realistic is to believe that the Afghan people will be impressed by our packets of peanut butter and pop-tarts, dropped from airplanes, and that they will thank us, and view us as their beneficent saviors. To be naïve is to point out that the food drops—according to relief agencies—are insufficient to meet the need, especially since our bombing has aggravated the refugee crisis to staggering proportions. To be really naïve is to note that to even get the food, Afghans would have to traipse across minefields, and might be blown to bits before they can even reach our humanitarian goodies. To be naïve to the point of disloyalty, would, I suppose, be to ask whether or not American soldiers in Pearl Harbor would have felt better about the bombing of December 7, 1941, had the Japanese pilots made a second run to drop sushi and edamame.

Perhaps it's just me. But something seems dangerously Alice in Wonderland, when Clinton advisor Dick Morris can say on national television that we should declare war on Afghanistan, and then Iraq, Libya, Sudan, and Colombia—and not be viewed as a paragon of mental illness—but Quakers and pacifists are derided as uninformed boobs.

And yet I have no doubt that many of these American warlords will attend Martin Luther King Jr. Day celebrations come January, and sing the praises of a man who would have condemned them roundly for their current course of action. And they will continue to go to church—those who call themselves Christians—and sing praises to someone whose teachings run completely counter to everything they are now doing. But hey, King, Gandhi, Jesus: what did they know? Dreamers all of them: naïve, simplistic, innocent, and not nearly as informed or clear-headed as say, Donald Rumsfeld, or Stephen Ambrose, or Tom Clancy, or White House spokesman Ari Fleischer.

Even more disturbing than the uniformity with which conservatives have labeled dissenters un-American and unrealistic (which at least is to be expected), is the rapidity with which so-called progressives have accepted the need for, and ultimate propriety of war. Richard Falk—a longtime international peace expert—has called Operation Enduring Freedom, "the first truly just war since World War II." This, despite the fact that by the standards he himself has laid out for a just war, the bombing of Afghanistan—and the refugee crisis alone that it has sparked—completely fail the test of justice.

Or *Nation* contributor, Marc Cooper, who suggests that antiwar protesters suffer from self-hate, and who accuses us of claiming that the U.S. invited the attack, merely because we point out that certain of our policies might have something to do with the motivation for flying 757s into buildings. The difference between explanation and excuse apparently having escaped him, and the good counsel on a Thesaurus that might explain the difference apparently being out of his reach. Cooper insists that the left should embrace limited military action (the substance of which he leaves undefined) as a "moral imperative."

Perhaps most perplexing is the stance taken by Eleanor Smeal, of the Fund for the Feminist Majority. Recently she testified to Congress about Afghanistan, not to plead for an end to the macho militarism currently underway, which is likely to accelerate the starvation of thousands of women and girls there, but merely to suggest that the women of Afghanistan not be forgotten in any reconstruction government. Not only does she appear to support the overthrow of the Taliban by the same U.S. government that funded it and cared not a whit for the women there until six weeks ago, but she also seems to trust that patriarchy can be pounded into rubble by exploding phallic symbols, dropped and fired by guys whose view of feminism is probably not much better than Mullah Omar's. To suggest that there is any way to reconcile this war with feminism or the interests of women generally strains credulity, especially given the propensity for gang rape so well developed among our new "contras," the Northern Alliance. Talk about irony.

Again, maybe it's just me. Or maybe it's 1984, and War *Is* Peace, and Slavery *Is* Freedom, and Ignorance *Is* Strength. Or maybe all that is just bullshit, being served up on a silver platter, while the servers tell us it's really Goose Liver Pate. It reminds me of something my Grandma once said: "You can call your ass a turkey, but that doesn't make it Thanksgiving." Likewise, you can call your war just, and the rest of us naïve, but that won't make it so.

International Appeal of Nobel Prize Laureates, Poets, Philosophers, Intellectuals and Human Rights Defenders for an Immediate End to the War against Afghanistan

(2001)

Military measures intended to support the arrest of a terrorist have turned into a large-scale attack on one of the poorest countries in the world, as well as on its population, which is tormented by hunger and poverty and threatened by uprooting and death.

As little as the gap between rich and poor in the world was the cause of the murderous attack on Sept. 11, all the more are the attacks against Afghanistan deepening this gap and thereby multiplying reasons to hate the West and its civilization. In the future the West will be less identified with its best qualities, with democracy, a constitutional order and prosperity than with its shadowy sides, with a lack of respect, arbitrary acts and violence.

With every bomb that falls and every western soldier who kills on Afghan soil, the rich part of this world closes its eyes to the suffering of the peoples in the south. Even the apparent successes presently do not change this. With its offensive the West is not only undermining the idea of a collective legal effort to counteract terror, but is also betraying its own principles. In the final analysis this undeclared war is no longer being waged to combat terrorism but rather to preserve a reputation of military invincibility. Finally, with every day that war is waged there and with every new security law passed here (in the western world), that very freedom which is supposedly being defended is threatened and those refugees, who are the products of this military action and its consequences, are marginalized.

On September 11, not only did thousands of people suffer an agonising death, but even western civilization suffered a defeat. Those murdered in the attack will not be restored to life through the war against the Taliban. With every day of war the risk of a still greater moral and political disaster increases. It is still possible to learn from the failures experienced up to now. There is still a chance to return to negotiations and to reach a political solution which attempts to reestablish a legal order and to provide for justice and social equality in Afghanistan and in the world.

13th November, Frankfurt (Germany)

First Signatories:

José Saramago (Portugal, Nobel Prize in Literature 1998)
Günter Grass (Germany, Nobel Prize in Literature 1999)
Adolfo Pérez Esquivel (Argentina, Nobel Peace Prize 1980)
Rigoberta Menchú Tum (Guatemala, Nobel Peace Prize 1992)
José Ramos-Horta (East Timor, Nobel Peace Prize 1996)

Adonis (Ali Ahmad Sa'îd Esbir) (France/Lebanon)
Orhan Pamuk (Turkey)
Mahmoud Darwisch (Palestine)
Ogaga Ifowodo (Nigeria)
Harold Pinter (Great Britain)
Faraj Sarkohi (Iran)
Juan Villoro (Mexico)
Abdourahman A. Waberi (Djibouti/France)
Sean McGuffin (Ireland)
Christa Wolf (Germany)

Uri Avnery (Israel)
Monseñor Samuel Ruiz García (Mexico)
Danielle Mitterrand (France-Liberté, France)
Dr. Paz Rojas Baeza (CODEPU, Chile)
Akin Birdal (Human Rights Defender, Turkey)

Dr. Jean Ziegler (Delegate of Suisse to the United Nations)
Günter Gaus (Germany)

Prof. Giorgio Agamben (Italy)
Prof. Neville Alexander (South Afrika)
Prof. Francis A. Boyle (USA)
Prof. Judith Butler (USA)
Prof. Hajo Funke (Germany)
Prof. Axel Honneth (Germany)
Prof. Walter Jens (Germany)
Prof. Steve Lukes (Great Britain/Italy)
Prof. Jean-Luc Nancy (France)
Prof. Bertrand Ogilvie (France)

All possible care has been taken to obtain permission from the copyright owners to reprint the articles and selections protected by copyright. Any errors or omissions are unintentional and will be rectified in any future printings upon notification to the editors, who wish to express their gratitude for permission to reprint material from the following sources:

Daniel Berrigan/Thich Nhat Hanh: From *The Raft Is Not the Shore* by Daniel Berrigan, S.J. and Thich Nhat Hanh. Copyright © 1975 by Daniel Berrigan, S.J. and Thich Nhat Hanh. Reprinted by permission of Beacon Press, Boston.

Dorothy Day: "Pacifism" originally appeared in *The Catholic Worker*, May 1936, 8, and "Our Country Passes from Undeclared War to Declared War; We Continue Our Christian Pacifist Stand" in *The Catholic Worker*, January 1942, 1,4. Both pieces are reprinted by permission of The Dorothy Day Library (www.catholicworker.org/dorothyday).

Erich Fromm: "The Case for Unilateral Disarmament" by Erich Fromm reprinted by permission of *Daedalus*, Journal of the American Academy of Arts and Sciences, from the issue entitled, "Arms Control," Fall 1960, Vol. 89, No. 4.

Mohandas K. Gandhi: "My Faith in Nonviolence" by Mohandas K. Gandhi. Copyright © 1930 by The Navajivan Trust. Reprinted by permission of The Navajivan Trust.

Daisaku Ikeda/Linus Pauling: From *A Lifelong Quest for Peace* by Daisaku Ikeda/ Linus Pauling. Copyright © 1992 by Daisaku Ikeda and Linus Pauling. Reprinted by permission of Jones & Bartlett Publishers.

Martin Luther King, Jr.: "Declaration of Independence from the War in Vietnam," reprinted by arrangement with the Estate of Martin Luther King, Jr., c/o Writer's House as agent for the proprietor, New York, NY. © 1970 Dr. Martin Luther King, Jr., copyright renewed 1991 by Coretta Scott King.

Thomas Merton: "The Root of War Is Fear" by Thomas Merton from *Passion for Peace: The Social Essays*. Copyright © 1962 The Crossroads Publishing Company. Reprinted by permission of The Crossroads Publishing Company.

A. J. Muste: From *The Essays of A. J. Muste. 2001 Edition.* Edited and with an introduction by Nat Hentoff. Published by A. J. Muste Memorial Institute. Reprinted by permission of A. J. Muste Memorial Institute.

Arundhati Roy: From *Power Politics*. Copyright © 2001 by Arundhati Roy. Reprinted by permission of South End Press.

Jonathan Schell: From *The Fate of the Earth*. Copyright © 1984 by Jonathan Schell. Reprinted by permission of the author.

Henry A. Wallace: "Are We Only Paying Lip Service to Peace?," from *A History of Our Time*, 6/E by William Chafe and Harvard Sitkoff Beth Baily, Copyright © Oxford University Press. Used by permission of Oxford University Press, Inc.

Tim Wise: "Who's Being Naïve?" by Tim Wise. Reprinted by permission of the author. All rights reserved.

Howard Zinn: From *The Politics of History* by Howard Zinn. Copyright © 1970 by Howard Zinn. Reprinted by permission of Beacon Press, Boston. "Retaliation" by Howard Zinn. Copyright © 2001 by Howard Zinn. Reprinted by permission of the author. "Retaliation" appeared in a slightly different form in *The Progressive* magazine.